CLASSIC
CARVING
PATTERNS

CLASSIC
CARVING
PATTERNS

LORA S. IRISH

The Taunton Press

COVER PHOTO: Scott Phillips

Taunton
BOOKS & VIDEOS
for fellow enthusiasts

First printing: 1997
Printed in the United States of America

A FINE WOODWORKING book

FINE WOODWORKING® is a trademark of The Taunton Press, Inc.
registered in the U.S. Patent and Trademark Office.

The Taunton Press, 63 South Main Street, PO Box 5506,
Newtown, CT 06470-5506

Library of Congress Cataloging-in-Publication Data

Irish, Lora S.
　　Classic carving patterns / Lora S. Irish.
　　　　p.　cm.
　　"A Fine woodworking book" — T.p. verso.
　　ISBN 1-56158-173-9
　　1. Wood-carving — Patterns.　　I. Title.
　　TT199.7.I75　1997
　　736'.4 — dc21　　　　　　　　　　　　　　96-46958
　　　　　　　　　　　　　　　　　　　　　　　　　　CIP

CONTENTS

In memory of my father,

H. Ralph Cunningham
(1924–1995),

an old whittler
from way back

INTRODUCTION

As a freelance artist, I've always felt it important to keep a file of designs and project ideas that I've completed. This file, or artist's morgue, is a record of work that I've done as well as a source of reference that I can draw on for future works. When I began carving wood several years ago, it was natural to start compiling a file of patterns specifically for woodworking. As with most craftspeople, one idea often creates several variations and those variations expand into new ideas. This book is a sampling of those ideas.

You will find within these pages detailed drawings of patterns made for wood, which you can use for carving, burning, or painting. The detailed pencil sketches will help you visualize the final dimensions of your carving or the shading line of your painting. With each drawing, there's a larger outline pattern of the design that you can use for transferring to your own project. (Depending on the scale at which you're working, you can use the patterns at the size shown or enlarge or reduce them on a copier.) Although the designs are clearly created, it will be your imagination that will transform them into fine furniture and other heirloom creations.

Many of the designs contain reference marks that will direct you in squaring the pattern to your work or a center mark for compass placement on circular designs. Also included at the end of the book are a few tips on pattern making and design transfer.

Whether you're looking for a small accent or a large panel pattern, a corner or a curve, I hope that this book will help to spark your imagination.

1

PATTERN THEMES & SHAPES

Throughout history, carving patterns have tended to follow a group of general themes. These themes include geometric and repetitive pattern themes, natural pattern themes, the human form and face, fantasy pattern themes, and storytelling pattern themes.

GEOMETRIC AND REPETITIVE PATTERN THEMES

Some of the earliest designs that artists created were based on repeating circles and spirals, chevrons, and line work. The simplicity of a banded line or a beaded edge is still used today as a primary accent to furniture making. Repetitive lines and geometric patterns establish a rhythm throughout the entire form. The skilled use of a routed edge or a fine inlaid line of contrasting wood can transform a simple furniture

design into a classic work of art. Chip carving is a wonderful example of the use of repetitive pattern. Basic triangles magically transform into elaborate circles, diamonds, and squares that capture the viewer's attention with their depth and highlights.

By creating a single unit of work and carrying that design throughout the form, you can capture the interest of the viewer. This style of artwork is very simplistic, and each area of enhancement is predictable. Just as it is obvious that glassware of different sizes but with a repetitive design belongs together, we can expect that furniture with a repetitive theme will be used together in the same setting. When a piece of furniture is designed with two different elements, such as a bookcase mounted on a desk, a repetitive design unites the elements into one complete piece.

REPETITIVE
GEOMETRIC
PATTERN
(see p. 21)

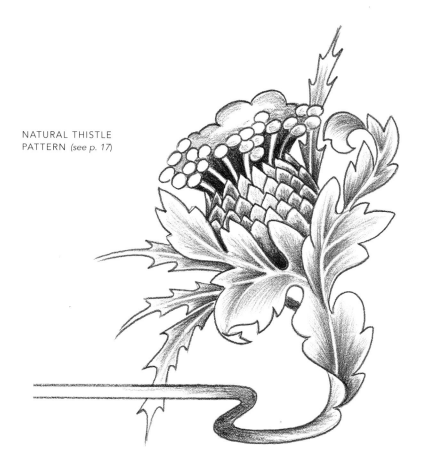

NATURAL THISTLE
PATTERN *(see p. 17)*

NATURAL PATTERN THEMES

The second general theme area for the carver is natural images. Leaves and flowers, birds and animals, and landscapes are everyday images that appear in ornamentation. Given that nature allows the artist the widest range of ideas, it is not surprising that this is the largest category of design themes.

Natural artwork often identifies the region where the art was created. The thistle design is commonly associated with artwork from Scotland, while the cherry-blossom design is traditionally Japanese. The eagle and star pattern quickly brings the viewer to the American shores. Artists from different regions may even treat their interpretation of a design idea differently. An English artist may create a rose as a multipetaled semicircular flower with a simple center, whereas an American artist may draw the rose as a tightly wrapped cylinder with a few escaping petals.

Not only does the natural pattern help to establish where the art was made, but it can also identify when it was created. The nosegay pattern, a circular cluster of simple flowers that often includes violets, pansies, daisies, and wild roses, reflects the trend toward English-style flower gardens during the late 1800s. The acanthus-leaf pattern became popular during the 1600s and is still a classic carving theme today because of its flowing, expressive lines, its simplicity in carving, and its adaptability to different elements of furniture.

The hex sign and the distelfink pattern can quickly be dated to the 18th- and 19th-century Pennsylvania Dutch. Today this simple form of art has found new popularity in modern stencil work and primitive landscapes used on refinished furniture.

Natural themes may either be true to nature, as in modern decoy-carving work where each feather is carefully and accurately placed, or stylized, as in antique decoy work where only the most general impression of the form is carved. Both create decoys, yet each has its own feel and form.

HUMAN FORM AND FACE

Carvers have used the human form and face as a theme to reflect both mankind's ideas and emotions. In ornamentation, the human face, often male, can take on physical attributes from nature. Ram's and bull's horns lend a mythical, powerful feeling to the design. Hair, mustaches, and beards flow and interweave with leaves and branches to represent the

MYTHICAL HUMAN FACE *(see p. 150)*

FANTASY PATTERN *(see p. 143)*

mystery of nature. Angel wings and halos can lift the viewer to Heaven, while deer antlers and lion fangs added to a face show us man's darker side. Whereas geometric patterns and natural patterns allow carvers to deal with recognizable shapes or to copy the real world around them, patterns in the human form and face category encourage artists to explore mankind's fascination with nature.

FANTASY PATTERN THEMES

Fantasy images are often used to capture the unexplainable events or fears of daily life. Gargoyles, winged dragons, devils, and angels all show up on the carver's palette of ideas. Eastern dragons portend cataclysmic natural events, such as volcanic eruptions and earthquakes, but they can also be representative of good omens. During the Middle Ages, Western dragons represented man's dark side. Today, dragons show the mythical and fanciful nature of man.

Gargoyles are often the artist's way of poking fun at his fellow man. Here the carver can create a distinct impression in the viewer by exaggerating physical features and emphasizing emotional expression. Even though the gargoyle design appears to be a mythical animal, gargoyles are commonly shown in human poses doing human tasks.

STORYTELLING PATTERN THEMES

Many designs are used to tell visual stories. Scenes that include a retriever, quail, and pastoral background relate a tale about the excitement of the hunt. A country scene created with an old farmhouse and decaying barn may tell a story about the carver's feelings of home and roots. By using storytelling themes the artist can record man's daily life and activities. Each element of the story becomes united within the boundaries of the relief. Historically, storytelling themes have appeared in every area of artwork, from

STORYTELLING PATTERN *(see p. 146)*

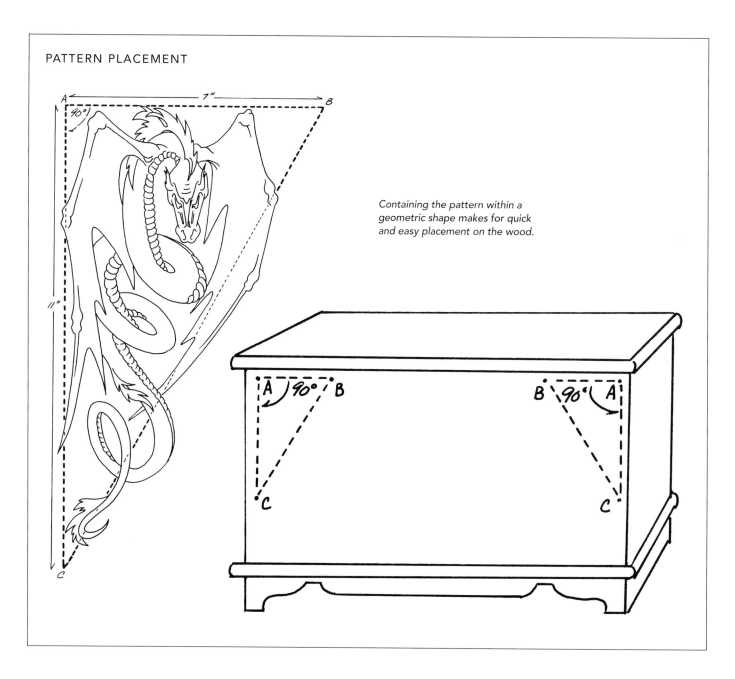

Containing the pattern within a geometric shape makes for quick and easy placement on the wood.

fresco and mosaic murals to small jewelry box lids. This pattern theme has a strong place in today's wood crafting, as reflected in the marvelous relief carvings and wood burnings that are currently being done.

BASIC DESIGN SHAPES

Many of the patterns used for wood carving, burning, and painting are free-flowing designs with branches, leaves, and floral accents. Planning the placement of these patterns on the wood can be difficult since there are few reference points that relate to the structure of the furniture. Establishing a general shape to the design, or determining the general area that the design will use, can make the planning of the final project

easier. Because a triangle has three straight sides and three definite angles it is easier to measure and place on the wood to be carved than a design of a dragon that has no definite or measurable boundaries. But if the dragon design can be contained in the general outline of a triangle and the triangle is used for placement marks, the dragon design can be readily transferred to the wood (see the drawing above).

Most designs fall into one of seven basic shapes: line, triangle, square and rectangle, circle and oval, S-curve and C-curve, mirror image, and free-form. All of these basic design shapes make use of lines, angles, and points that can be measured and easily transferred to the wood (see the drawing on the facing page).

BASIC DESIGN SHAPES

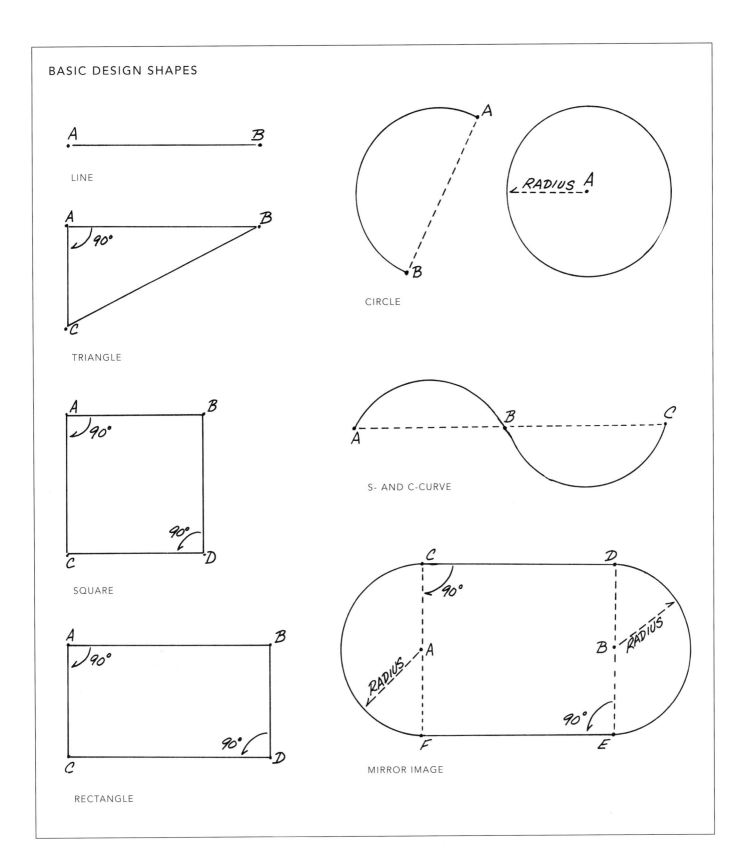

LINE

TRIANGLE

SQUARE

RECTANGLE

CIRCLE

S- AND C-CURVE

MIRROR IMAGE

LINE
(see p. 16)

Line designs, triangular patterns, and square or rectangular sketches accent the basic form of woodworking by following the line of the furniture's structural members. A straight line design used along the sides of a hutch door can create vertical lift, enhancing the height of the project. Used across the drawer fronts of a bureau, the line design will visually pull the eye along the full length of the drawer, making the bureau appear to be more expansive than it is.

The triangular design reinforces the joinery of the wood structure by placing emphasis on the intersections of the different elements that create the furniture. Triangular patterns visually strengthen the angles and corners. Whereas a line design will accent one plane, either vertical or horizontal, a triangular design can emphasize the corner points, bringing the eye to the perimeter of the structure's frame.

Square and rectangular designs draw the eye to individual areas of the wood structure. They focus the viewer on specific elements, such as door panels, box lids, and chest fronts, and reenforce the basic shape that is used in woodworking.

Circular and oval patterns give more emphasis to the design. These patterns directly oppose the structural shape of the project, creating a pleasing contradiction for the viewer. By pulling the eye away from the hard, static edges of the work, a curved pattern can soften the general appearance of the furniture.

TRIANGLE
(see p. 43)

RECTANGLE
(see p. 59)

CIRCLE
(see p. 77)

(see p. 59)
(see p. 77)

S-CURVE
(see p. 99)

MIRROR IMAGE
(see p. 113)

The S-curve and the C-curve are very free-flowing patterns that complement nature. These patterns open up the structural form by accentuating both the height of the project with one part of the design and the width with other parts.

The mirror image is a design shape widely used in woodworking. This type of pattern allows you to use an open, flowing pattern within the confines of an angular structure. By focusing the eye on a central line down the wood form, you can reach in any direction and accent any area. Once the central line is established, you can embellish the structure of the furniture with curving headboards and aprons.

Free-form scenes are open-edged designs that are self-contained by their interrelated elements. Here the structural element of the wood on which they are used creates the final shape of the design. Often the free-form pattern is marked from one line within the design. An example would be a reference line drawn from wing tip to wing tip on an American eagle design. Although free-form patterns may occupy the entire area of the wood, using a general reference line will make the placement of the pattern easier.

Although the seven basic shapes may seem to cover a wide range of possible designs, there will always be one design that just does not seem to fit into any category. Remember that the basic shapes are used only for planning the final look of the design on the furniture and for easier placement on individual wood pieces. The basic shape will not be carved or burned—it is only for reference. Therefore, when a design does not fit into a general shape category, you can choose an arbitrary shape that overlays the design. This arbitrary shape now provides the reference points for measuring.

Some designs fit more than one category. In the chapters that follow, I've grouped the patterns by basic design shape, but there is a certain amount of overlap. Don't be surprised to find a mirror-image design in the chapter on line designs, or even a circular pattern in the chapter on squares and rectangles.

FREE-FORM
(see p. 152)

✿ 2 ✿
LINE DESIGNS

From a simple beaded line to the complex interlacing of grapevines, line designs create visual movement across the face of the furniture. By accenting one direction, either vertical or horizontal, you can move the viewer from one structural element to another while emphasizing either the height of the work or the length.

Simple beaded lines, roundover edges, and ogees are basic woodworking enhancements. You can expand these straight line designs with a natural or geometric element. By adding a small overlay to the basic line, you can create areas of emphasis for the viewer. Corners, drawer handles, and central points are excellent areas to add a visual surprise.

Line designs are also made up of repeating units, which make it easy to create designs of a given length that will match the structural form. Repetitive units create a visual ruler for the viewer, a way to mark the size of the form. When using repetitive units the final look of the line design can be changed by reversing the units at the central point, by reversing the pattern every unit, or by mixing different sizes of units throughout the line.

Mirror-image line designs keep the free-flowing shape of natural elements while pulling the eye away from a central point on the structure. This type of design may be changed throughout the work by inverting the mirror image from one structural area to another.

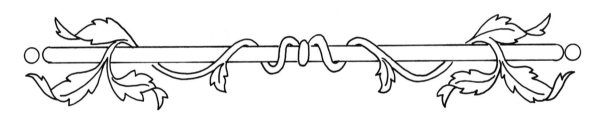

BEADED LINE

REPETITIVE LINE

MIRROR IMAGE

Line-design patterns need not be composed of straight lines only. Using a flowing or curving line can soften the final effect of the furniture and still give vertical or horizontal emphasis. Adding a gentle curve or loop to the main line of the pattern breaks any long expanses across the structure (see the drawings below).

To place a line design on the wood for carving, burning, or painting, you need to establish a reference line through the pattern and determine the length of the line design. The reference line can be used to ensure that the pattern is parallel to the edge of the wood element. To center the design, first subtract the length of the pattern from the length of the wood

element. Then divide this measurement in half to find the distance the design needs to be placed from either side of the wood element (see the top drawing on the facing page).

Line designs work well on table aprons and trestles, hutch valances and toeboards, molding-strip areas, drawer fronts, and the stiles or rails along door fronts. When using a line design, choose one main direction for the pattern. This keeps the viewer's eye moving easily up and down or back and forth across the form. If the pattern changes direction, it can be visually confusing and make the finished piece seem disconnected.

Line designs created with gently curving elements can be confined within parallel reference lines for placement.

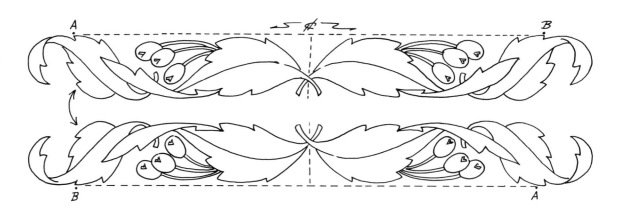

The addition of holly leaves and berries softens what would otherwise be a static, crisp line across the surface of the wood.

LINE-DESIGN PLACEMENT

To place a line design with accuracy, mark a straight line through the pattern and register it to a corresponding line on the wood structure.

Line designs emphasize the length of individual elements within the wood structure. Here, the beaded line that connects the acorn designs pulls the viewer's eye across the expanse of the drawer fronts.

HOLLY SWAG

OCTOBER BERRIES

OAK AND ACORNS

STYLIZED THISTLE

SINGLE-LEAF END

TWISTED-LEAF OVERLAY

SCROLL END

TRIPLE-LEAF END

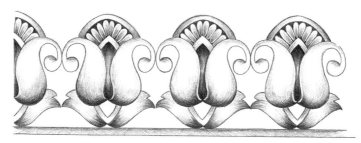

STYLIZED TULIPS

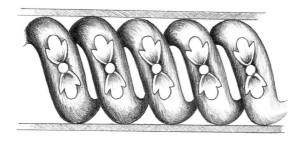

PATTERNED TWIST

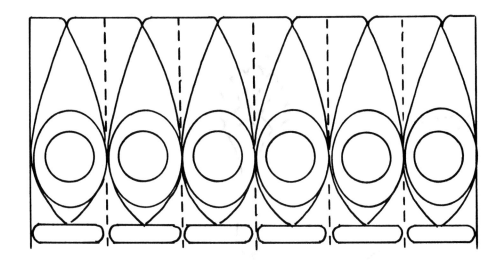

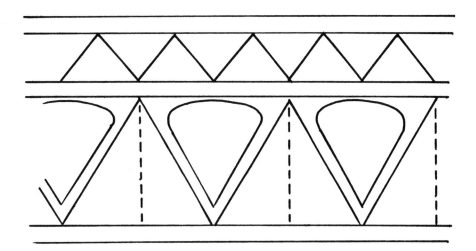

TEARDROPS

ARROWHEADS

WROUGHT-IRON TWIST

SPLIT STYLIZED TULIP

IRON HEART

HALF-DAISY TURN

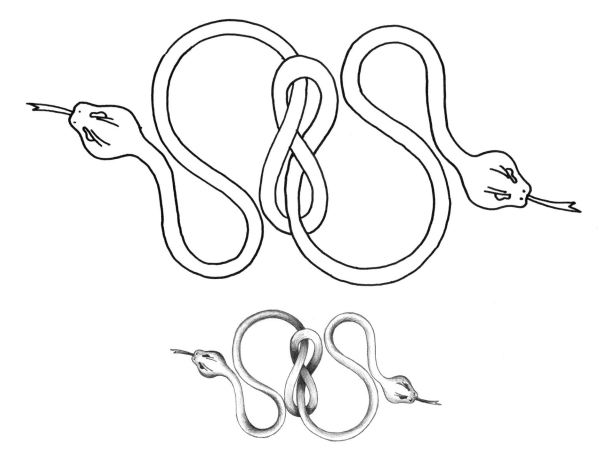

KNOTTED SNAKE

IRON-LEAF CIRCLES

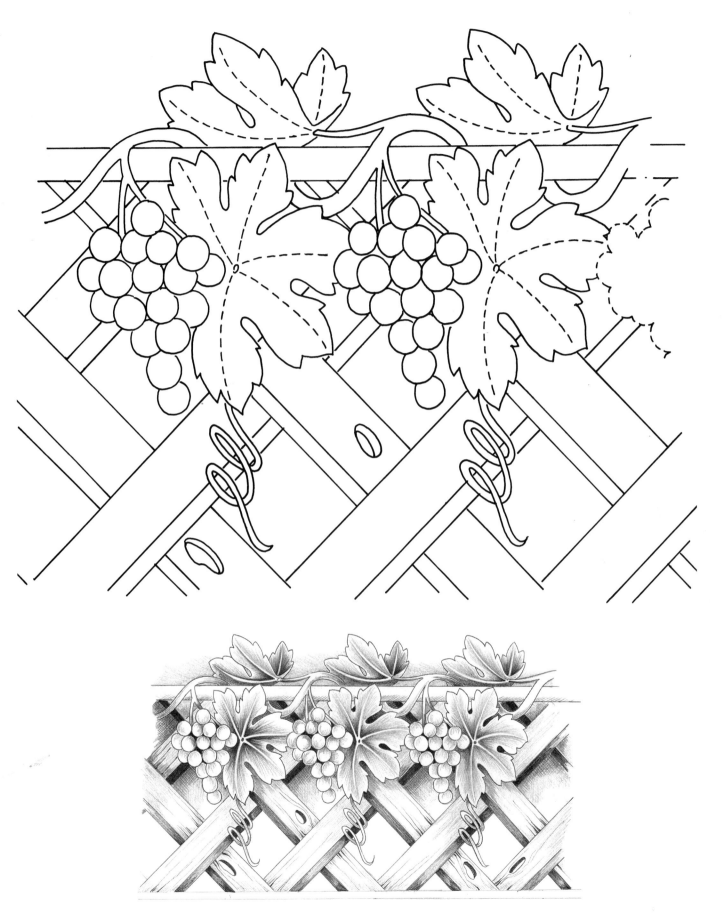

HARVEST LATTICE

POD AND PETAL LATTICE

POD AND PETAL LEAF

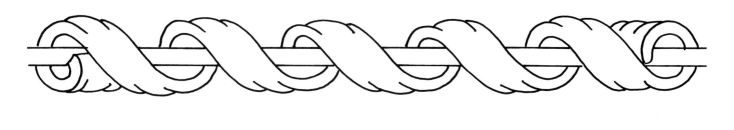

RIBBON AND BEADED LINE

✿ 3 ✿
TRIANGULAR DESIGNS

Whereas line designs emphasize the vertical or horizontal structure of the wood form and square designs bring the focus to the repetitive rectangles of the furniture, triangular designs draw the viewer's eye to the corners of the work. By using this pattern style, the vertical supports of the woodwork are united with the horizontal structures.

The corners and right angles of a piece of furniture are areas of joinery, either where two pieces of wood come together or where two separate units of the furniture form are in contact. These areas are ideal for pattern work. A triangular design visually pushes against the corner in which it is placed. This thrust can be used to accent the final size of the piece by focusing on the four corners of the form. Height can be accentuated by using triangular patterns along only the top edge of an element.

In woodcarving, the triangular pattern can be extended into lattice and pierce-work additions to the final furniture form. Along the upper corners of an open-front hutch, carvings that fit into the right angles not only enhance the shelf area with design but also seem to support the hutch top.

Not all triangular patterns must have three straight sides. A pattern that is created with one right angle can have an inner side that curves, thereby breaking the crisp, angular feel of the design. This feature makes the triangular pattern an excellent frame for circular or oval designs (see the drawing at right). A circle pattern might be used on the door panels with a triangular pattern that has a curved side in the corners of the door frame (see the drawing on p. 30).

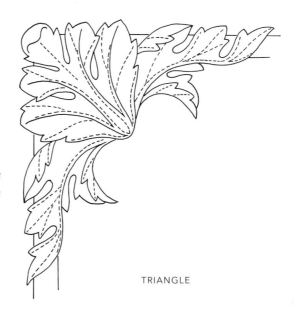

TRIANGLE

TRIANGLE AS FRAME

To transfer a triangular pattern to the wood, use the lines of the right angle and a measured point along each side as reference marks. These marks can easily be measured from the right angle on the wood elements. Once the pattern is marked, it can be inverted from top to bottom on the furniture or reversed from side to side (see the drawing on the facing page).

Since most triangular designs are used in the corners or right angle of the wood form, a word about joinery is appropriate. When choosing the furniture piece or area to enhance, consider the joinery used in the wood structure before you begin your pattern work. Dovetails, finger joints, inlaid joints, and some forms of Japanese joinery are decorative in themselves. Pattern work should complement the final form not compete with it. Placing a pattern or design over a highly detailed piece of joinery de-emphasizes both the pattern and the joinery and creates a visually confusing area to the viewer. Remember that fine joinery work is in itself an art and does not need an accent.

Equally important, do not use a pattern to try to conceal poorly constructed joinery. If there is a problem with the original joint work, the problem will still be there underneath the pattern and design work. In this case, the viewer's eye is drawn to the very area that you wish to minimize. It is better to recut the original joinery than to try and hide it.

CREATING A "FRAME" WITH TRIANGULAR DESIGNS

The triangular patterns used in the corners frame the central circular designs and unite them with the rectangular shape of the door panels.

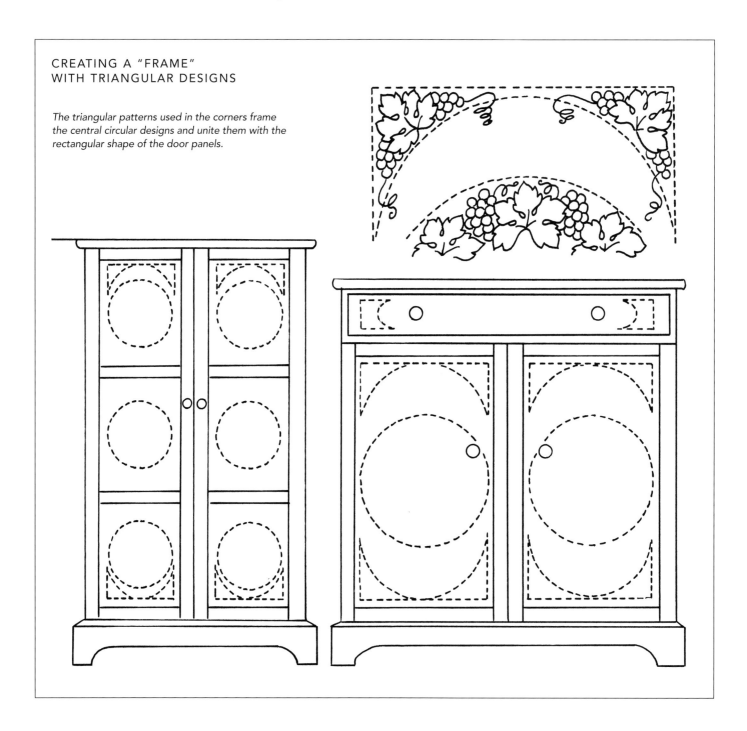

TRIANGULAR-DESIGN PLACEMENT

Even though the size and orientation of the design work may vary from one wood element to the next, using the same geometrically shaped pattern in each area maintains continuity throughout the piece.

POINSETTIA ROSETTE

MARASCHINO CHERRIES

FLUTED SHELL

VICTORIAN LEAVES

ROSE-LEAF CURL

BASKET WEAVE

REMBRANDT TULIPS

CATHEDRAL CORNER

ARCHED ACANTHUS

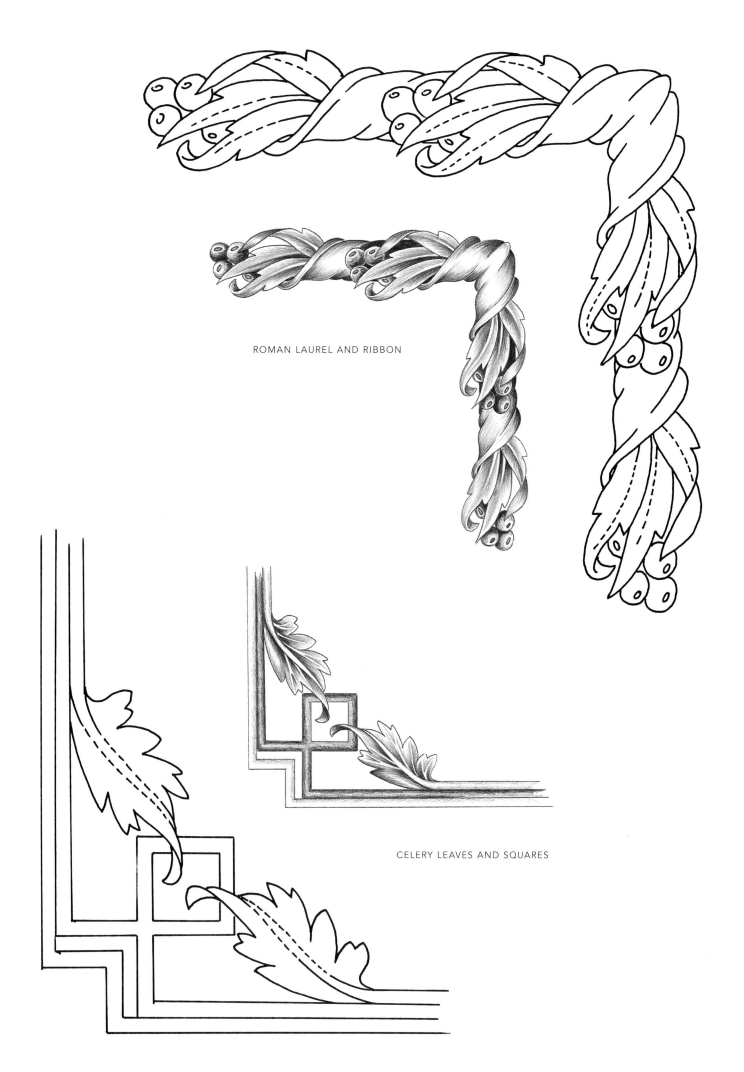

ROMAN LAUREL AND RIBBON

CELERY LEAVES AND SQUARES

TWIST AND TURNS

SUMMER ROSES
(outer corner)

HERALDRY LEAVES

SIMPLE ROSE

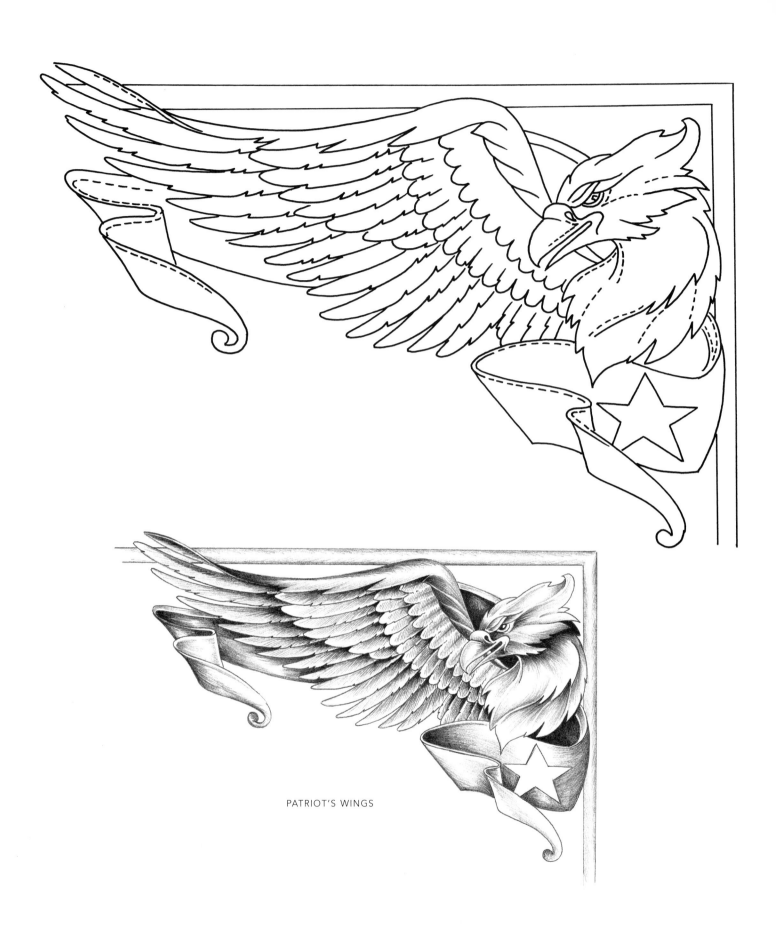

PATRIOT'S WINGS

LEATHER AND LATTICE

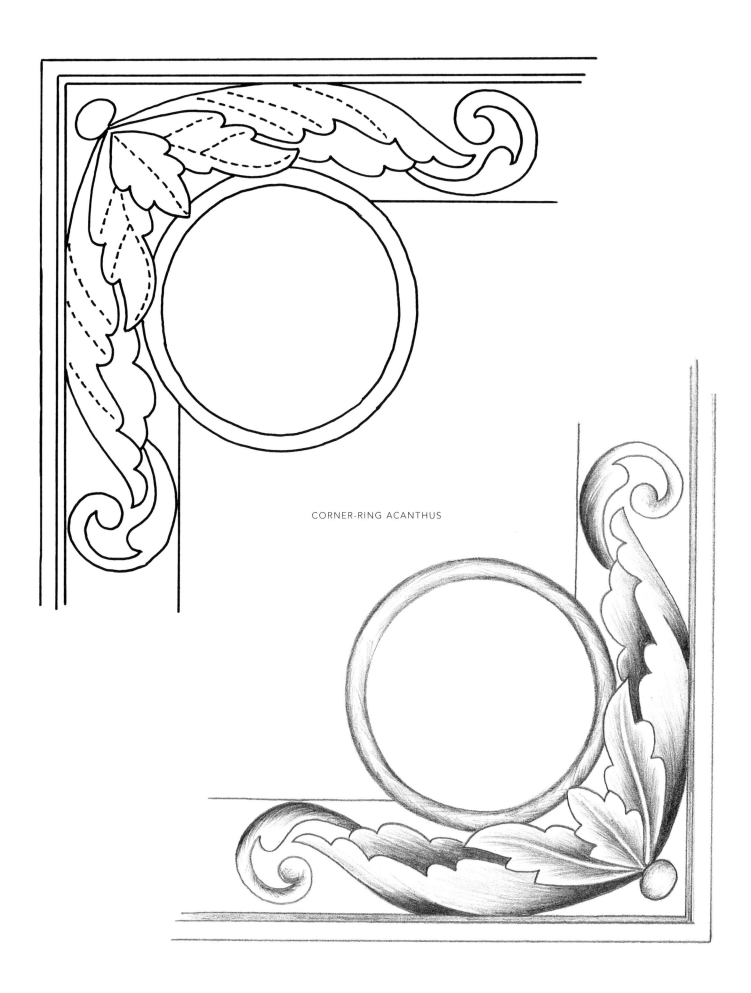

CORNER-RING ACANTHUS

SUMMER ROSES
(inner corner)

4

SQUARE & RECTANGULAR DESIGNS

Line designs readily change into square or rectangular designs simply by turning the corner. These designs allow you to take the pattern along the perimeter of the structure and emphasize the box forms of the furniture (see the drawing at right). By using an even margin along each side of the square or rectangular design, the size of the element on which the pattern is used is visually strengthened.

Turning the corner with a line design can be accomplished in several ways. First, you can allow one element of the line design to touch the same element at the 45° line in the corner (Drawing 1 at right). Since this configuration will reverse the pattern at the corners, you'll need to compensate by finding the center point of each side segment and flipping the pattern over to direct it toward the next corner.

A second way to turn the corner is to continue the pattern in one direction through the corner intersections (Drawing 2 at right). In this design, one element at the beginning of the pattern always touches one element at the end of the pattern, and every pattern segment is laid down in the same direction.

Using a square or rectangular design emphasizes the structural lines of the furniture.

1   2   3

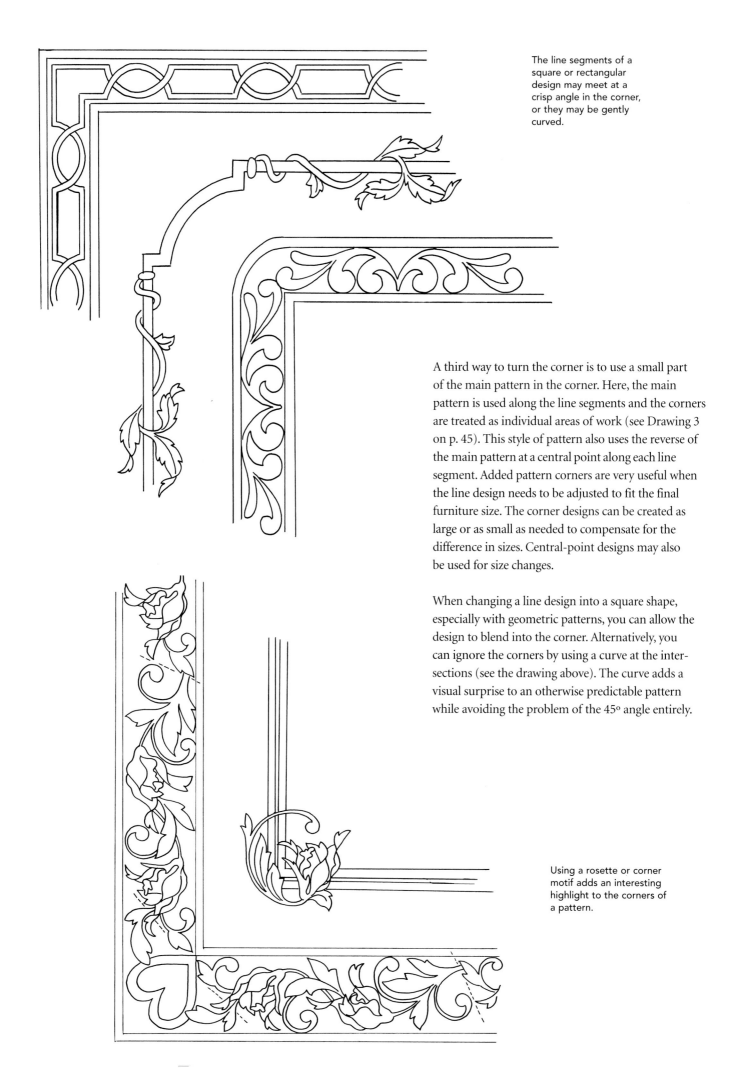

The line segments of a
square or rectangular
design may meet at a
crisp angle in the corner,
or they may be gently
curved.

A third way to turn the corner is to use a small part
of the main pattern in the corner. Here, the main
pattern is used along the line segments and the corners
are treated as individual areas of work (see Drawing 3
on p. 45). This style of pattern also uses the reverse of
the main pattern at a central point along each line
segment. Added pattern corners are very useful when
the line design needs to be adjusted to fit the final
furniture size. The corner designs can be created as
large or as small as needed to compensate for the
difference in sizes. Central-point designs may also
be used for size changes.

When changing a line design into a square shape,
especially with geometric patterns, you can allow the
design to blend into the corner. Alternatively, you
can ignore the corners by using a curve at the intersections (see the drawing above). The curve adds a
visual surprise to an otherwise predictable pattern
while avoiding the problem of the 45º angle entirely.

Using a rosette or corner
motif adds an interesting
highlight to the corners of
a pattern.

Rosette designs can be created to fill the corner areas of a square design. Just as in a door frame, the rosette in design work joins a vertical design to a horizontal design with a corner pattern or motif. This pattern may be part of the line design used in the general pattern work—as in the frame of the lion drawing below where the corner motif repeats the curve of the geometric units—or it may be something completely different. An example of the latter would be a beaded line that uses a rosebud pattern to highlight the corner, or a line design of wild roses with a heart design in the corner (see the bottom drawing on the facing page).

Square and rectangular designs are sometimes used to contain free-form patterns, just as a picture frame contains or surrounds a painting. In this type of format the design reaches out to the edges of the square but does not go beyond its lines; for example, the lion pattern below is captured within the boundaries of the geometric design.

A square or rectangular design can be used to frame a free-form pattern.

Triangular patterns can be combined to create a square shape. Repeating a triangle in each of the four corners and allowing the patterns to connect along the sides gives the final appearance of a square or rectangle (see the drawing at right). Also, working with the triangular pattern laid along the diagonal axes of the square can create a balanced, four-sided shape (see the drawing above). For some ideas on how to use these designs on furniture, see the drawing on p. 50.

Square and rectangular designs are extremely complementary to woodworking because they reflect the basic shape of furniture elements (see the drawing below). They may be used to accent door panels, chest lids, and drawers. When determining the placement of a square or rectangular design, you must consider the difference in size between the edge of the wood and the edge of the pattern. The margins can be equal on all four sides, which will place the design centrally in the wood element, or they can be wider at the side or top and bottom edges. Making the side margins wider emphasizes the height of the wood element, whereas using wider margins along the top and bottom of the design accents the width of the furniture form.

Use the outer perimeter of the rectangle and its four corner points as reference marks when transferring the pattern. By marking the desired margins and the four corner points onto the wood element, you now have marks that correspond to the pattern.

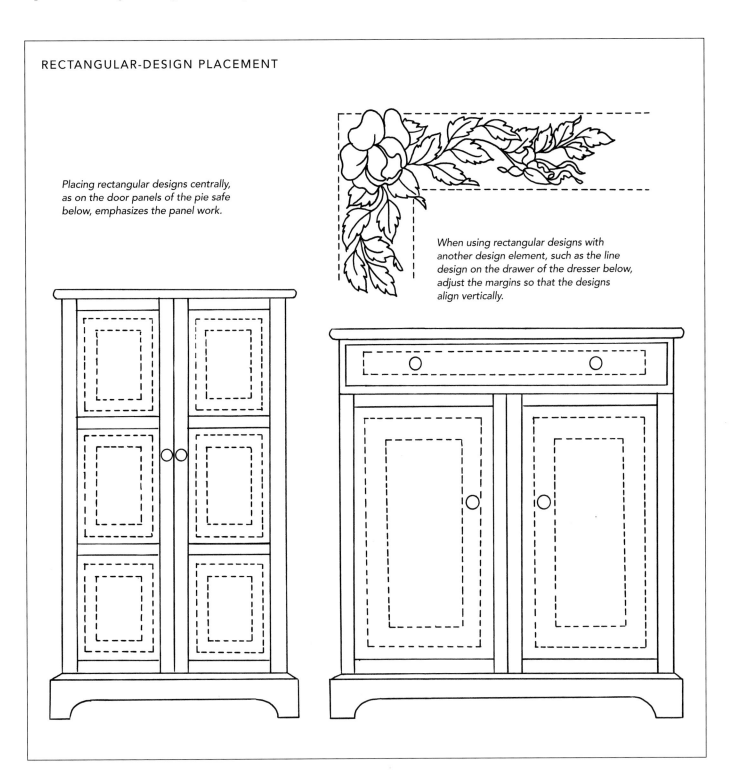

RECTANGULAR-DESIGN PLACEMENT

Placing rectangular designs centrally, as on the door panels of the pie safe below, emphasizes the panel work.

When using rectangular designs with another design element, such as the line design on the drawer of the dresser below, adjust the margins so that the designs align vertically.

TRUMPET-VINE CLOCK

ROLLED SHELL

REMBRANDT-TULIPS PANEL

LACE-LEAF CLOCK FACE

CARNATION-PILLOW PANEL

CELTIC-BRAID PANEL

SMALL FLORAL CLOCK

DIAMOND LEAVES

❧ 5 ❧

CIRCULAR & OVAL DESIGNS

When you use a circular or an oval design, the emphasis is pulled away from the angular lines of the furniture and brought to the soft curves that contain the design. This pattern style places more importance on the carving (or wood burning or painting) since it is created with boundaries that are not directly related to those of the structure on which it is placed. This gentle conflict between, say, the rectangle of a door panel and the oval of a leaf pattern that has been over-laid upon it is a dynamic combination.

The circular design automatically creates its own margins on the wood element, leaving the corners free of design. Because of the basic shape of the pattern work and the corner transition area between the pattern and the perimeter of the wood element, using a circular design can minimize the chance of over-powering the furniture with design work.

The circle around each of these farm scenes both frames the barn landscape and accents the curve of the leaf ribbon.

Leaving a circular design open along one edge helps it blend into the wood on which it is placed.

Whether to use a circle or an oval to contain the design is determined by the shape of the wood element on which it is to be placed. A well-balanced pattern will have equal margins in the corners of the structure. Therefore, rectangular doors visually require oval designs, while square panels call for circular patterns.

The artwork doesn't need to be contained completely within a circle. Using a half-circle along the top of the pattern and allowing the curved lines to blend into a rectangular shape at the bottom can give the work a very uplifting look. This technique works especially well to accent tall door panels or to break up long horizontal elements, as on a blanket-chest front (see the drawing below). Leaving part of the circle open to the wood element on which it is placed can blend the design into the wood (see the drawing at left).

BLENDING CIRCULAR AND RECTANGULAR DESIGNS

Curving one or both ends of a rectangular pattern can break the monotony of a rectangular design within a rectangular wood element.

By adding a curve to both ends of a rectangle, you can create an elongated oval design, as shown in the drawing above. Another way to use a circular pattern to modify a rectangular design is to add a curved line to the center of the rectangle, which serves to break up the angular feel of the structure (see the drawing on p. 64).

The corners that are created by using a circular design within a square wood element can be areas for additional design work. Left bare, the unworked space emphasizes the curve of the pattern within an angular wood element. Carved with a triangular pattern that contains a curved side toward the circle, the corners can accent the conflict between the two shapes. Here, a pattern that's complementary to the circular design can reinforce the transition from the softness of the curve to the crispness of the angular lines (see the drawing at right).

To place a circular design on the wood, begin by drawing diagonals between opposite corners to find the central point of the wood element. Using a compass, you can now establish the diameter of the circle to be used. Allow a margin around the pattern so that it doesn't extend completely to the edge of the wood. If the pattern work will include curved triangles in the corner, mark two circles from the central point, one for the main pattern and the other to define the curved inside edge of the triangular pattern. To ensure accuracy, whenever possible use a compass to trace the circles directly to the work.

On arched patterns that are made with a half-circle top that blends into a rectangle at the bottom, use the two right angles at the bottom of the design for placement. Allow an equal margin along all the sides and from the upper point of the circle.

Oval patterns may be placed by matching the centerlines of the pattern and the wood element. Again, allow equal margins at the upper and lower points of the oval for even spacing.

CIRCULAR-DESIGN PLACEMENT

Place circular designs centrally to draw attention to the design. Here, the circular design is artfully integrated with a rectangular design.

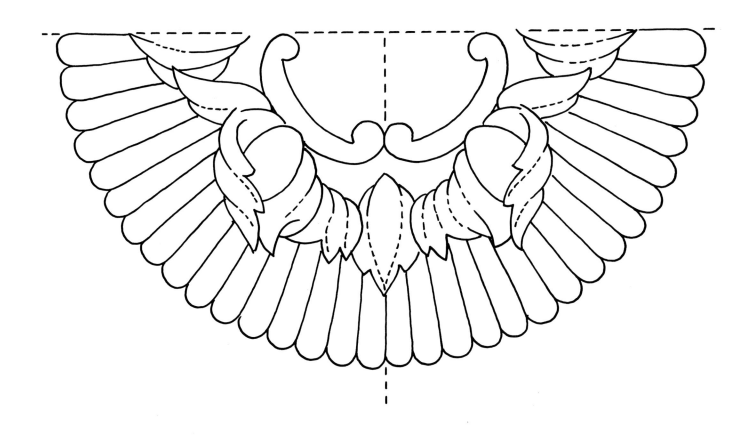

SHELL CIRCLE

HAY-BARN CIRCLE

MILKING-BARN CIRCLE

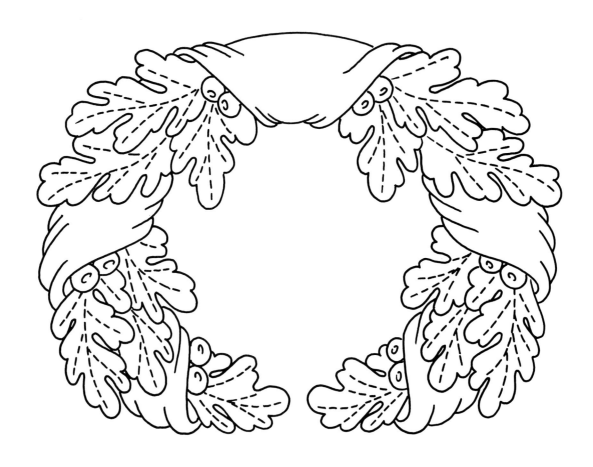

SMALL VICTORY WREATH

SWEETHEART OVAL

WROUGHT-IRON FEATHERS

VINE AND BERRIES OVAL

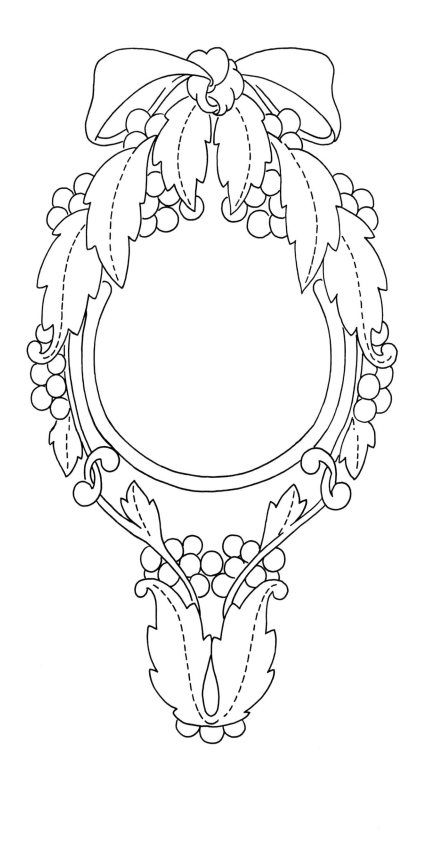

BOW AND BERRIES RING

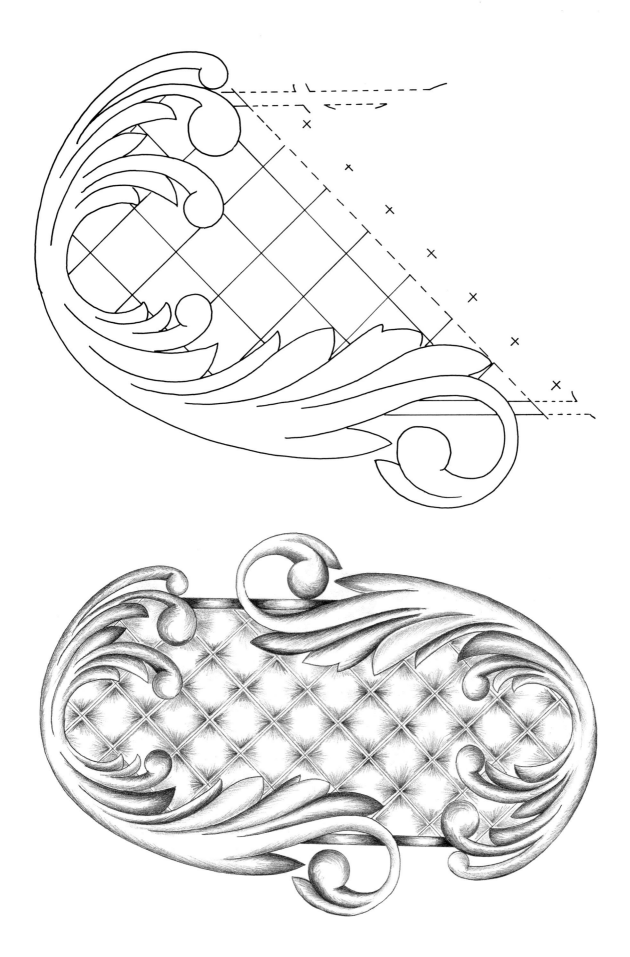

SCROLL-PILLOW PANEL

SIMPLE SCROLL

CURLED SWAG

WILD-ROSE CIRCLE

VINEYARD DELIGHTS

HARVEST CIRCLE

ROSE-ACCENTED FAN

TULIP OVAL

❋ 6 ❋
S- & C-CURVE DESIGNS

Of all the design shapes that can be used in wood-working, the S-curve and the C-curve are the most complementary to nature. With these designs, the pattern flows from one area of the wood element to another without a formal line to control it. This sense of flow makes S-curve and C-curve patterns ideal for

designs that are created with leaves, flowers, berries, and branches. S- and C-curves allow you to accent whichever part of the piece you wish. Whereas circular designs soften the look of the furniture, curved patterns free it from its harsh angular look as they seem to float across the surface (see the drawing below).

S- AND C-CURVE PLACEMENT

Using a central curved pattern can soften the impact of the repetitive angular lines inherent in furniture construction.

Most curved designs are worked as mirror images from the central line of the furniture. For example, if an S-curve is placed on one half of a drawer front, it would be reversed on the other half to maintain a balanced look (see the drawing above). Curved patterns may also be used on door panels to create a reflection of each other. Here, a C-curve or an S-curve may be placed facing the central rail between the doors, and the reverse of this curve may be placed on the opposite door to create a heart shape between the doors (see the drawing at left).

Scroll and ribbon designs also fall into the curved pattern category. Here, the flow of the line is determined by the flow of the scroll across the structure. This style of pattern is ideal when you want to include

Curved designs can be worked as mirror images from the central line of the furniture (top), or they can be used on adjoining panels to create a heart-shaped pattern (above).

Scroll and ribbon designs can be personalized to commemorate anniversaries and other events.

Simple curves create a flowing movement through the design.

writing within the design. Names, dates, or records of personal events become part of the design instead of an addendum to the pattern work. Including such personalizations in the design emphasizes their importance since the design is obviously created to commemorate this information (see the bottom drawing on the facing page).

To maintain the gentle flow of the pattern, try to keep the curves simple, as shown in the drawing above. Too many curves can be confusing to the viewer. Your goal is to create the soft feel of a gentle ocean wave, not the wild ride of a roller coaster.

When placing curved patterns on the wood structure, handle them as if they were straight-line designs. Find a straight line directly though the center of the pattern that allows an equal amount of design to either side of the line for balance (see the drawing at right). On this line establish two points, one toward each end of the pattern. The line and the two points may now be transferred to the wood structure, allowing easy placement of the pattern.

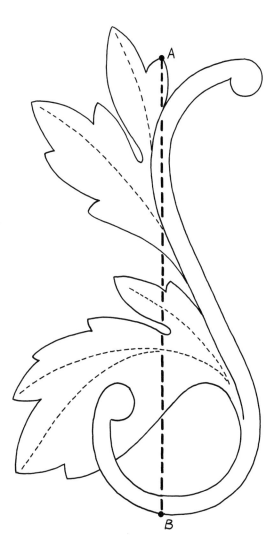

Curved designs may be placed on the wood from a vertical line centered through the pattern.

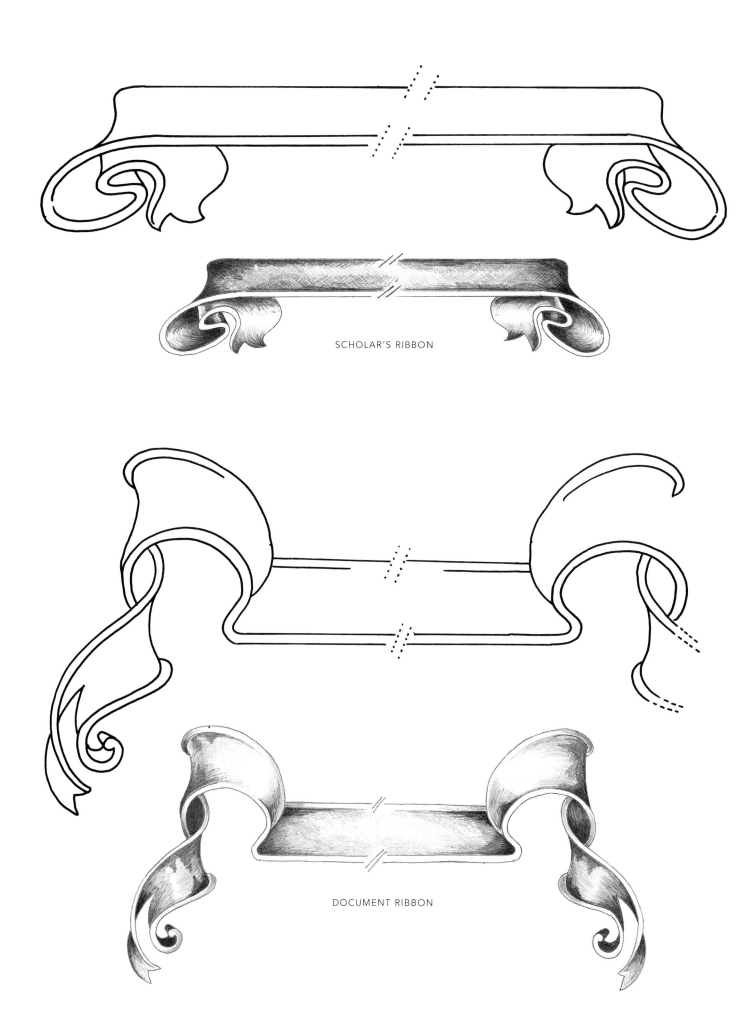

SCHOLAR'S RIBBON

DOCUMENT RIBBON

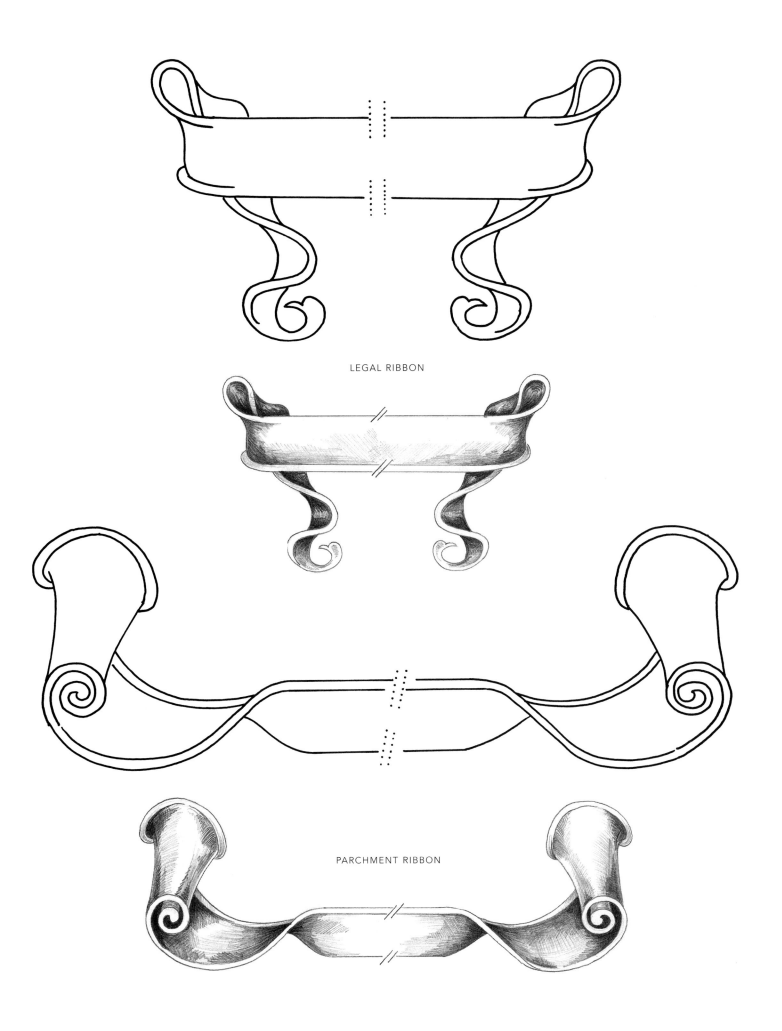

LEGAL RIBBON

PARCHMENT RIBBON

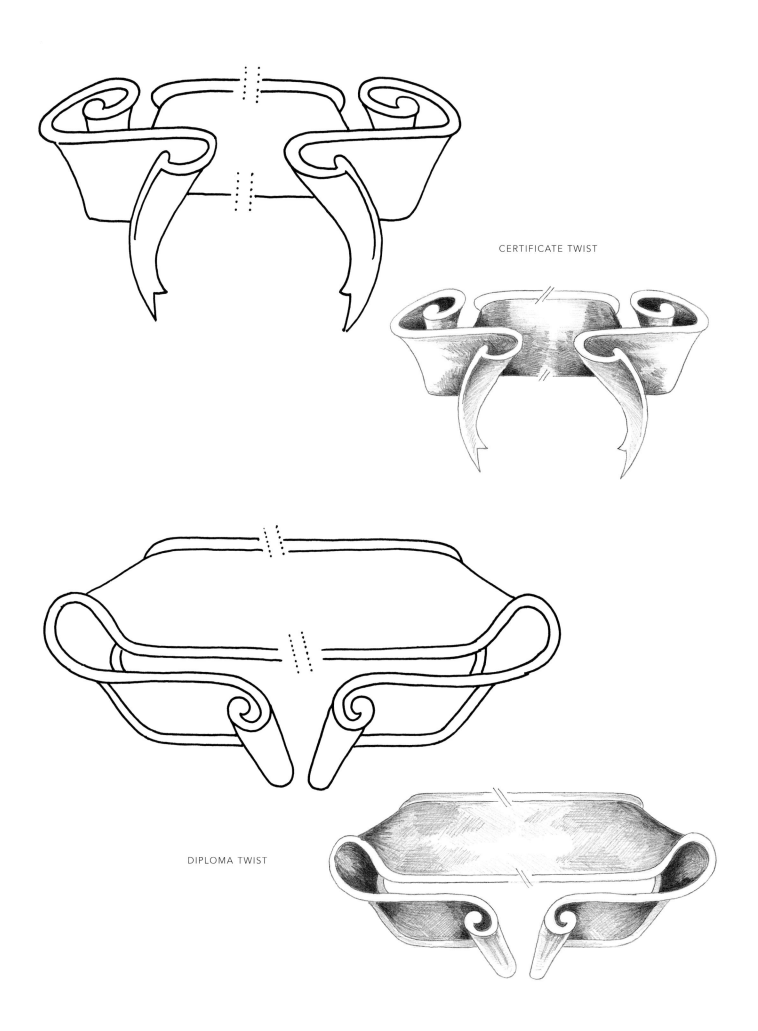

CERTIFICATE TWIST

DIPLOMA TWIST

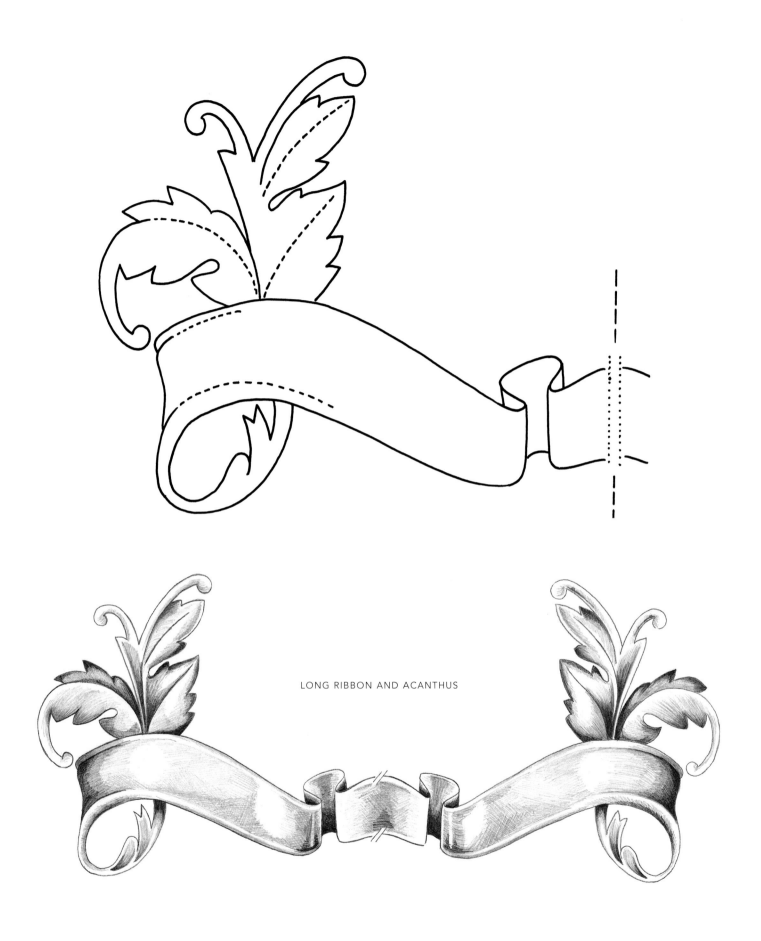

LONG RIBBON AND ACANTHUS

POMEGRANATE

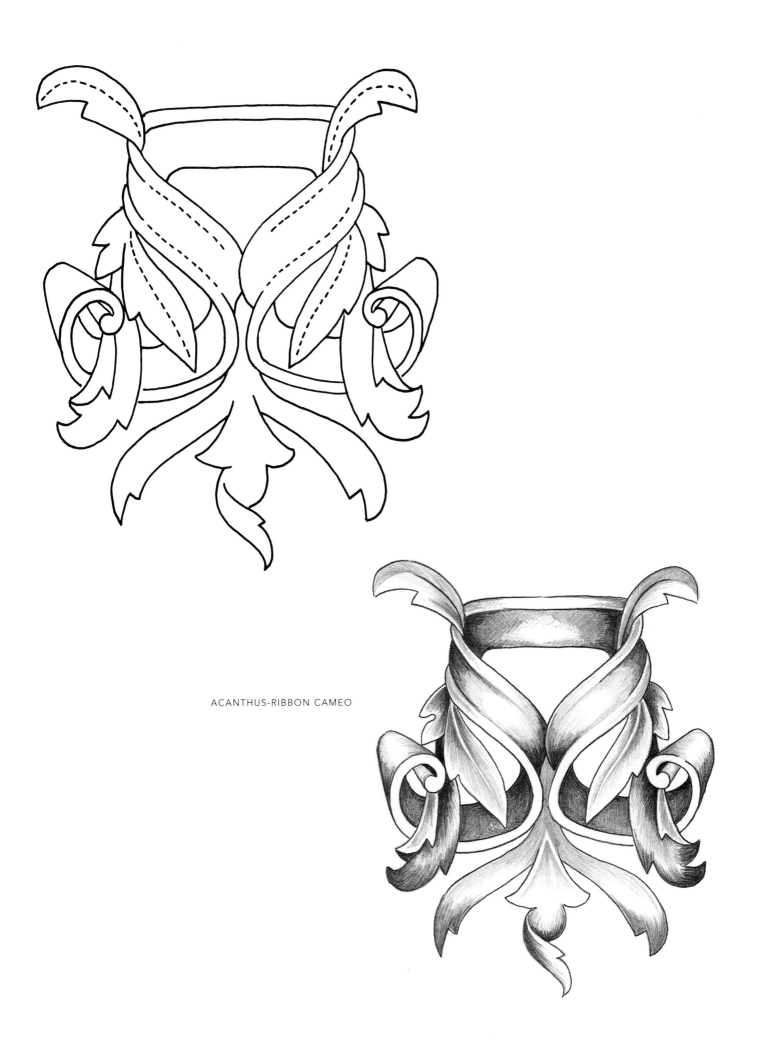

ACANTHUS-RIBBON CAMEO

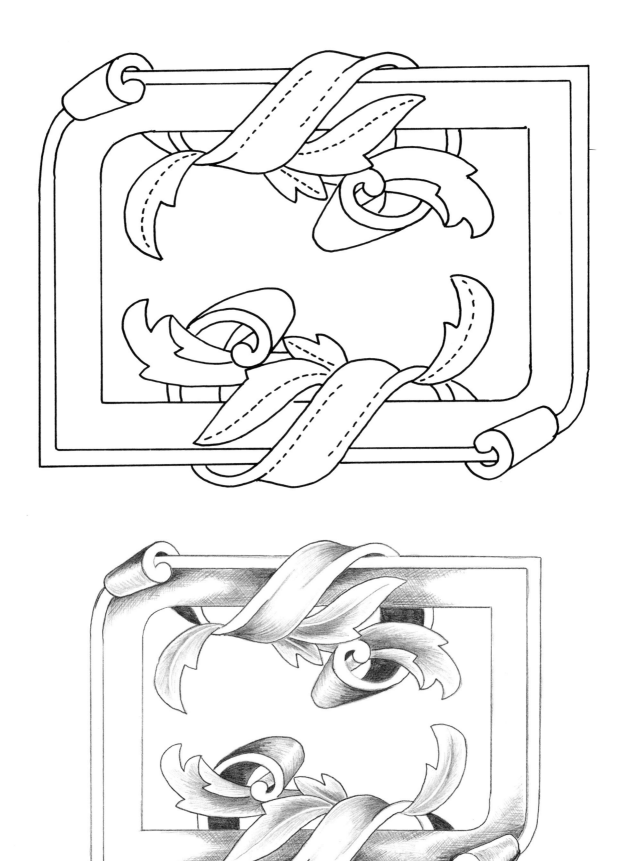

ACANTHUS-RIBBON FRAME

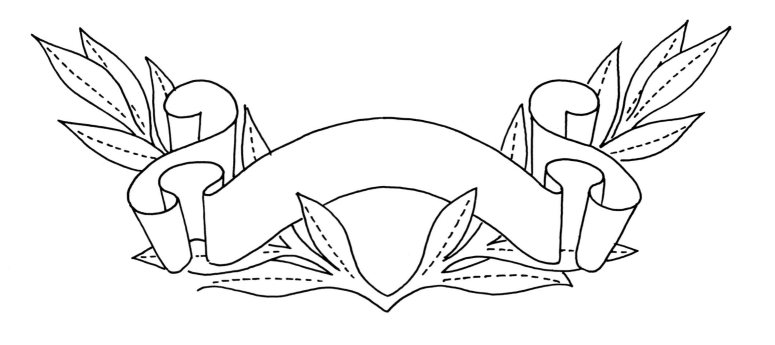

OLIVE-BRANCH SCROLL

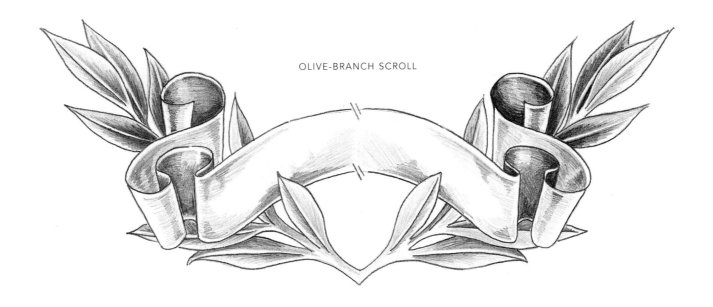

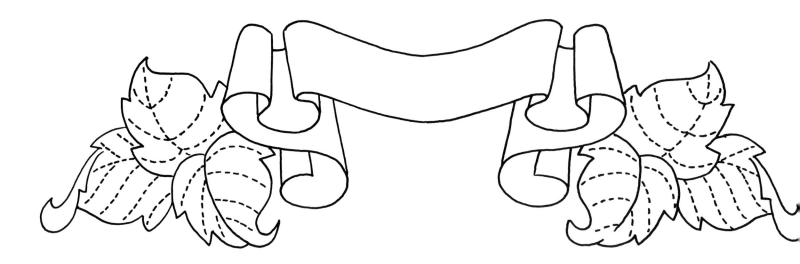

MULBERRY-LEAF SCROLL

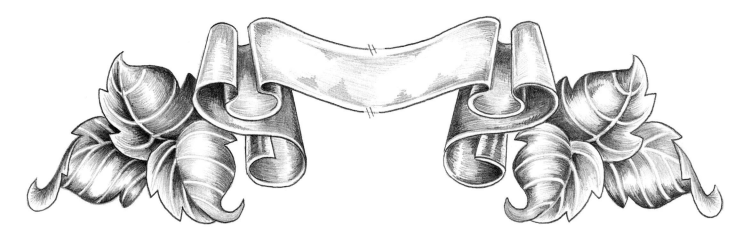

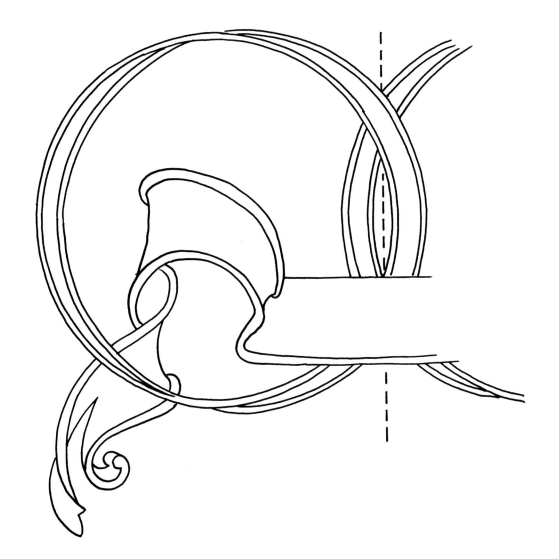

WEDDING-BANDS SCROLL

SEPARATED-PETALS SHELL

NINE-POINT SHELL

WINTER WHEAT

POMEGRANATE AND LEAVES

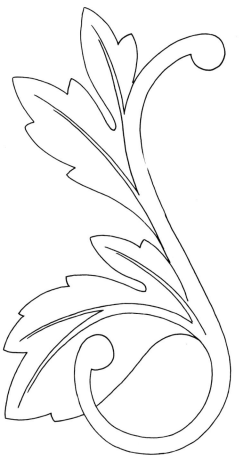

LARGE S-CURVE LEAF

LEAF AND SEED SHELL

SINGLE-SHELL LINE

LONG-SHELL CENTERPIECE

TRIPLE-SHELL LINE

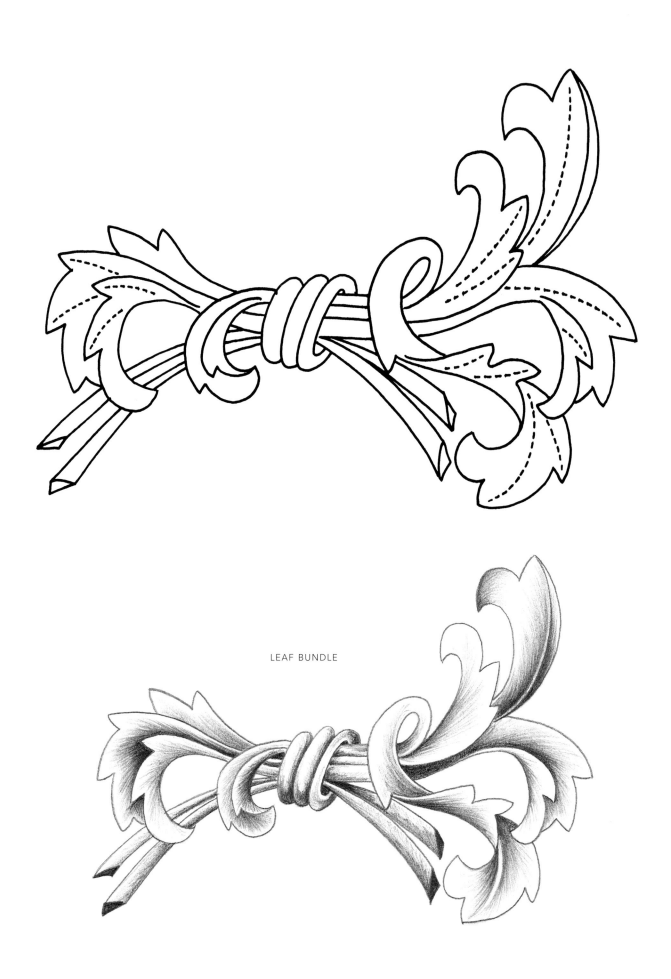

LEAF BUNDLE

BACK-TURNED LEAVES

CENTER LINE

LARGE HEART
TEMPLATE

90°

❃ 7 ❃
MIRROR-IMAGE DESIGNS

Of all the designs used in woodworking the mirror image lends itself most readily to large, creative expanses of artwork. Working from a central line, either vertical or horizontal, the pattern reaches outward across the face of the structure, repeating itself in reverse on the opposite side of the form. As with line designs and square designs, mirror images complement the basic structure of wood furniture.

A mirror-image design is created exactly as the name implies. One half of the pattern is drawn and then held against a mirror to see how it looks with its reflection. Using the mirror makes it possible to view the design work in progress and more easily direct the design. When the first half of the pattern is complete, a reverse tracing can be made to create the mirror reflection of the artwork.

Worked from a central line, the mirror-image pattern creates two identical sides to the design that are reflections of each other.

You can use any of the basic design shapes to create a mirror-image design: S-curves and C-curves, line designs, and triangular designs all work well. For example, making a mirror-image design from a triangular pattern allows you to use the larger design in one area of the structure and accent it with the single triangle designs in other areas.

Centerpiece designs also fall within the mirror-image category. These classic patterns, which include shell designs, vases, and garlands, are often used as accents on highboys and other pieces of furniture.

Since the mirror image is so obviously worked from a central line, a cameo pattern is sometimes added at the line to break the reflection. An example is the three-leaf cameo added below the ring in the design on the facing page.

To empasize the vertical lift of a piece, place the mirror image along the central line of the form. This placement works well for furniture designs that include tall doors or long, vertical panels. A mirror-image design may also be placed along the horizontal lines of the furniture form. Repeating a mirror-image pattern from drawer to drawer on a highboy can visually expand the width of the form while emphasizing the drawer work.

MIRROR-IMAGE PLACEMENT

Mirror images may be placed from a horizontal centerline to emphasize the height of the furniture (left), or they may be worked from a vertical centerline to emphasize the furniture's width (right).

TRIPLE-LEAF ACANTHUS WITH RING

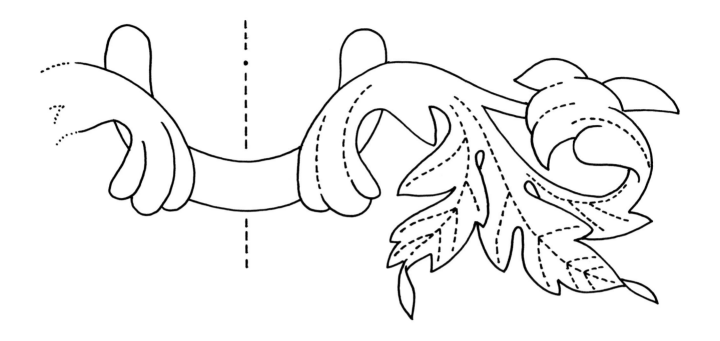

OPEN-CENTER HALF RING

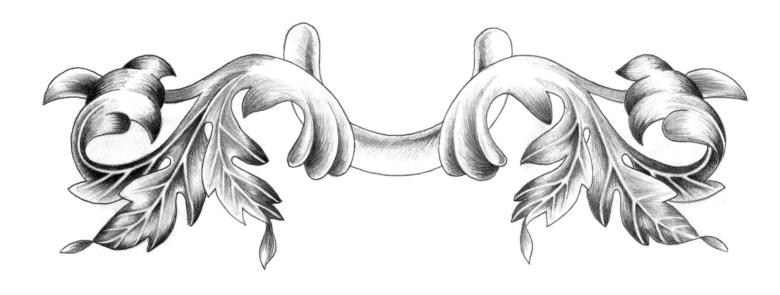

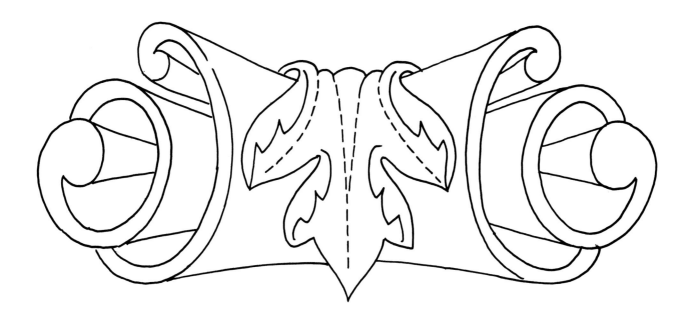

LEAF AND SCROLL

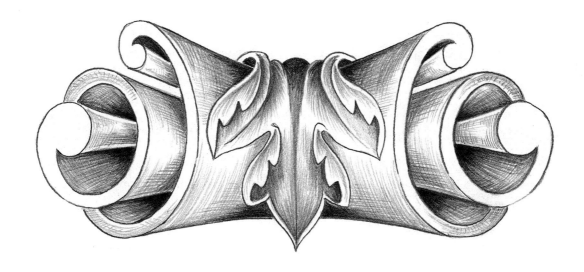

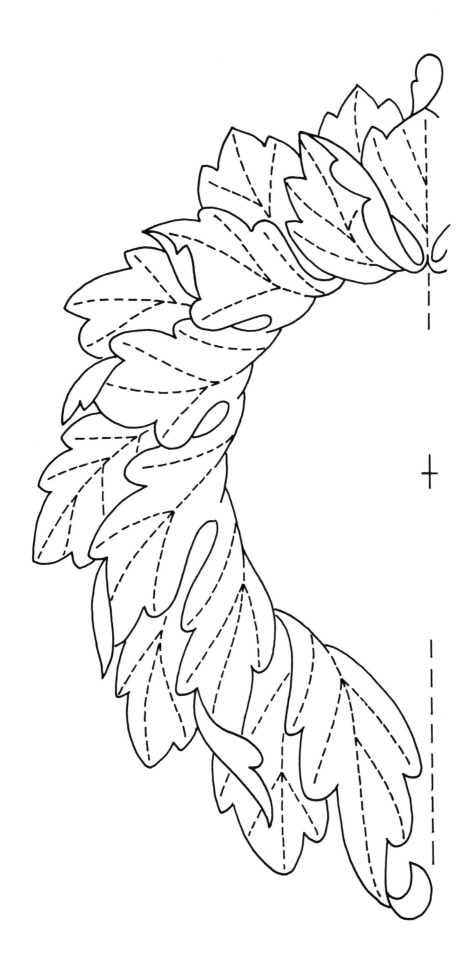

VICTORY-WREATH CENTERPIECE

CAPITAL COLUMN

QUEEN'S-CROWN LEAVES

DOUBLE CURVED ACANTHUS

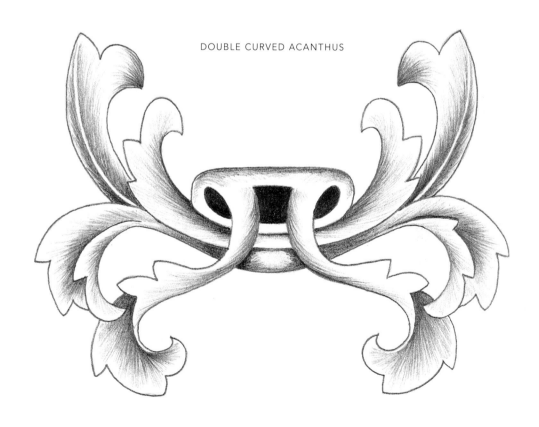

INTERLOCKED CRADLE HEARTS

BISHOP'S-SQUARE LEAVES

ROYAL-RIBBON I

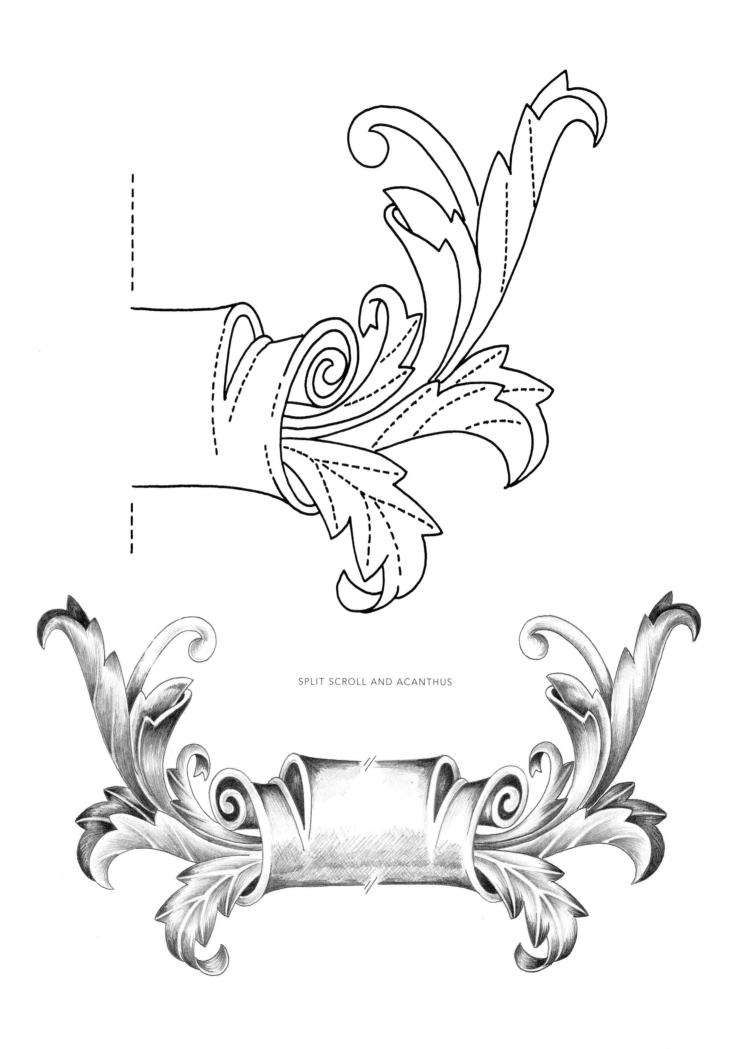

SPLIT SCROLL AND ACANTHUS

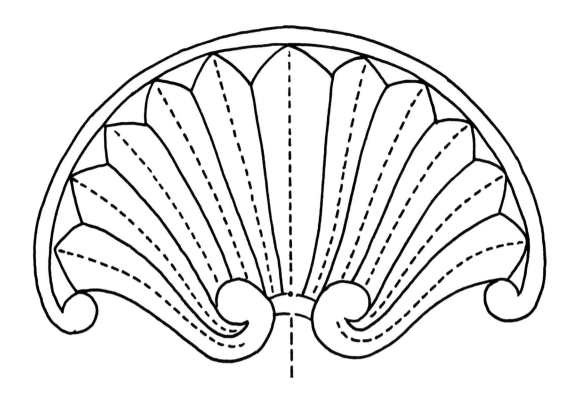

CLASSIC SHELL

SMALL HEART

LARGE HEART

LAUREL GARLAND

CORNERS AND CURLS

LILAC AND POPPY COMPOTE

WICKER BASKET

WINE-CHEST CORNICE

HIGHBOY SHELL

ROSE AND LAUREL SPRAY

CLASSIC CORNICE

OPEN-ROSE URN

8

FREE-FORM DESIGNS

While many patterns are used to accent and complement the furniture on which they are placed, free-form designs are typically created to tell a story, either about the elements contained in the design or about the intended user of the piece. Storytelling through artwork is one of the oldest forms of expression.

Drama, emotion, and intrigue can all be found in a free-form design. The brier-patch rabbit shown below scurries through the grass, his body in full motion. From where has he come and where is he going?

The hunting falcon (see pp. 146-147) has been unhooded by his trainer, yet he is still tethered to the branch. He waits, tense and with wing feathers ruffled for his final release to the hunt. The traditional eagle and flag (see p. 152) shows another majestic bird in a free-form design. The eagle is shown proudly displaying his long wingspan. His head and chest curl over the flag in a protective posture, his expression one of determination. The feelings of strength, courage, and protectiveness are quickly identified by the viewer in this patriotic pattern.

The human face is blended with nature to create the North Wind image.

Caricatures, such as this gargoyle waterspout, playfully overemphasize certain areas of the human form.

Carvers and wood burners sometimes create fantasy patterns within the free-form design category. For example, North Wind designs are traditionally used to blend mankind and nature, as seen with the addition of spiraling horns and the leaf wreath to the ram's-horn North Wind at left. Artists occasionally poke fun at the human situation by creating caricatures that overemphasize certain human features, as shown in the drawing of the gargoyle waterspout below. Dragons and other mythical creatures may be used to show feelings of anger and power (see the drawing on the facing page).

A good way to place a free-form design onto the wood element is to use a bottom line of the pattern that corresponds to a bottom line of the wood. For example, the ground line under the rabbit on p. 141 makes a perfect reference line. Alternatively, the design can be contained within a border design as a square, rectangular, or circular shape and be transferred to the wood element as that shape (see, for example, the lion-corner pattern on pp. 144-145).

At the end of this chapter you'll find a number of cameos, beaded-line endings, and two complete alphabets, which can be used to accent and comple-ment many of the designs found throughout this book. Cameos may be used to highlight selected areas of the wood element, such as keyholes, table legs, and the corners of a panel door, or to break up a long beaded line at the center point. Beaded-line endings add an interesting detail at the end of a raised line, say, on the apron of a Federal card table. And letters, in the form of initials, names, sayings, and so forth, can be used to personalize your design work and to commemorate special events.

ANTIQUE SCROLL DRAGON

LION CORNER

HUNTING FALCON

BRIER-PATCH RABBIT

RAM'S-HORN NORTH WIND

GARGOYLE WATERSPOUTS

TRADITIONAL EAGLE AND FLAG

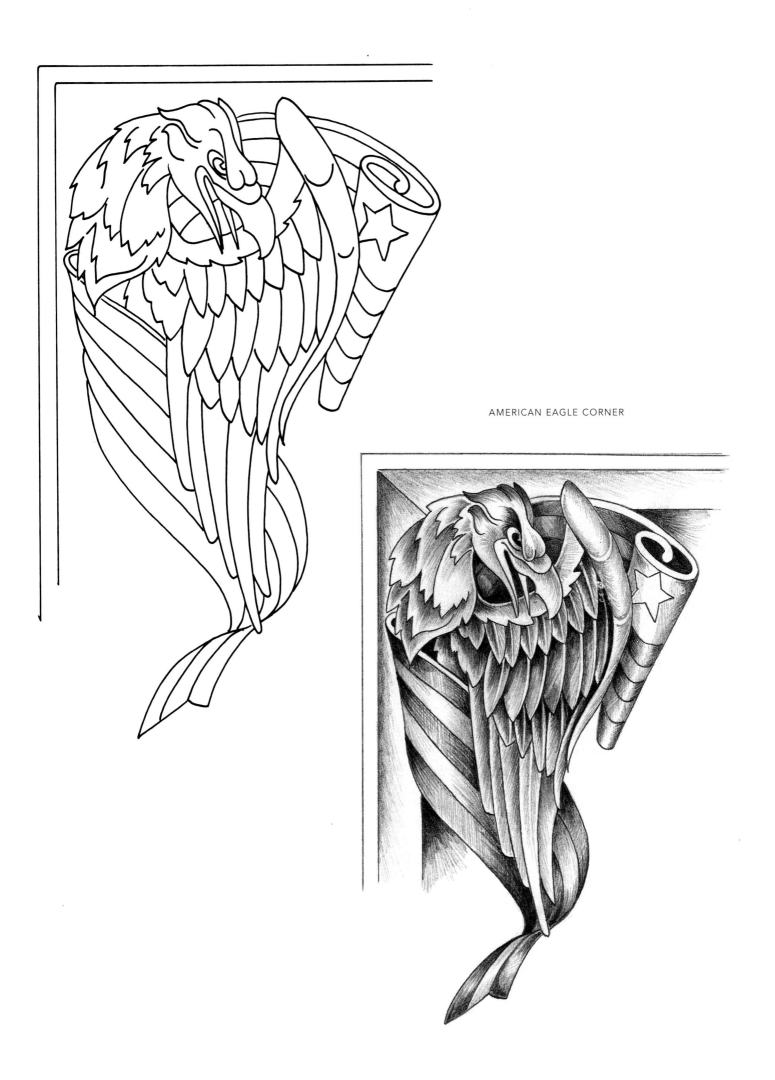

AMERICAN EAGLE CORNER

STARS AND BANNERS

BELLFLOWER CAMEO

BELLFLOWER RING

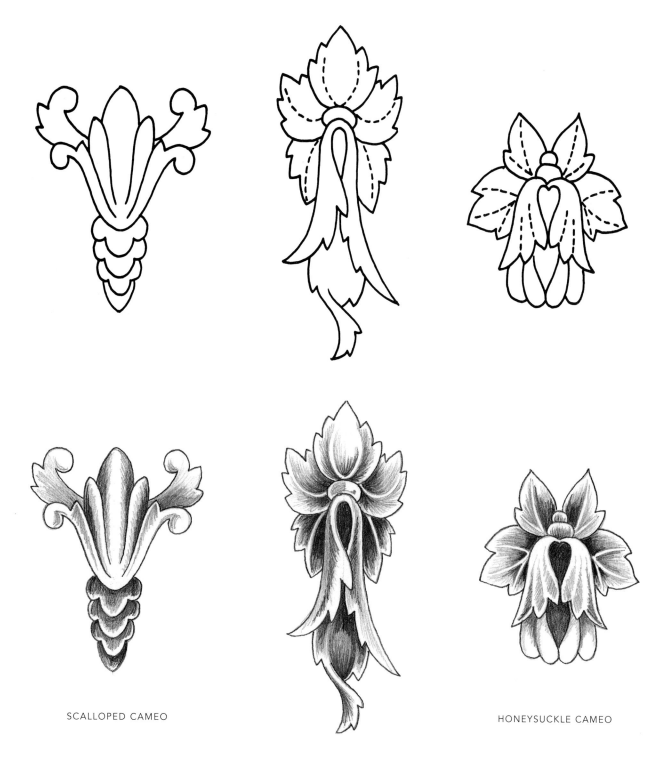

SCALLOPED CAMEO

SERRATED FLORAL CAMEO

HONEYSUCKLE CAMEO

CURLED-LEAF ACCENT

SHELL CAMEO

SIMPLE ROSE CAMEO

PETALED CORNER ACCENT

CIRCULAR LEAF ACCENT

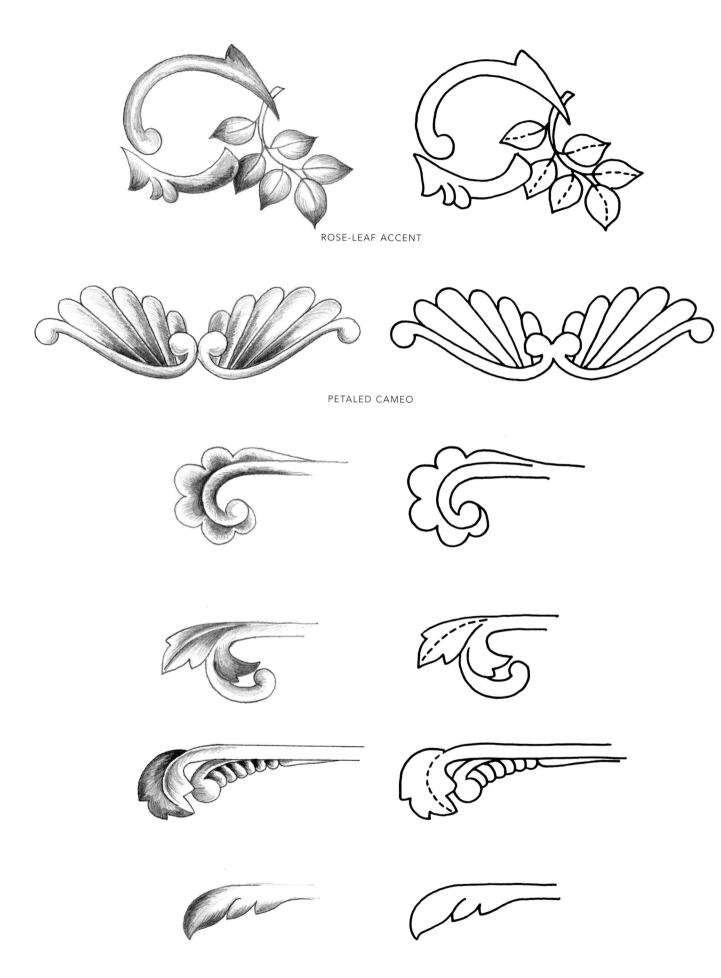

ROSE-LEAF ACCENT

PETALED CAMEO

BEADED-LINE ENDINGS

ABCD

EFGH

IJK

LMN

ROUND-SERIF ALPHABET

ROUND-SERIF ALPHABET

LEAF-CIRCLE MONOGRAM

LEAF-OVAL FERN

SCROLL-SCRIPT ALPHABET

SCROLL-SCRIPT ALPHABET

STENCIL ROSE

❦ 9 ❦

PLANNING & PLACEMENT

Deciding which pattern you wish to carve is just the beginning of the process that leads to picking up your carving knifes. You need to think about how the design will lie upon the wood and how it will affect the look of the furniture. This chapter considers the visual weight and the implied weight of the pattern and explains how to balance the two when placing the pattern on the wood. Also discussed is how to size a design to fit its area with the use of margins and air space.

Once you've sized the pattern, it's a good idea to test it on paper. Testing the pattern allows you to judge the overall effect of the carving on the furniture and make any adjustments before work begins. This chapter concludes with some ideas on how to move your chosen design onto paper and then transfer that paper pattern to the wood.

GRAPE LEAVES

The veining within the leaves, the curling tendrils, and the grapes within the cluster all add to the visual weight of this design.

VISUAL WEIGHT AND IMPLIED WEIGHT

Design work has two types of weight: visual weight and implied weight. When choosing a pattern to enhance a wood form, you need to consider both.

Visual Weight

Visual weight is determined by the space that the design occupies, the mass of the individual units within the design, the detail within each unit, and the air space that is captured by the pattern.

The grape-leaf design at top right fills its given space, reaching all the boundaries of the basic triangle. It is created with three massive units—two leaves and one cluster of grapes—each of which is highly detailed with either veining or individual grapes within the cluster. There is very little background within the design; what there is, is broken into very small areas. This pattern would be considered a visually heavy design.

Using a negative-image design, with the background darkened to show the amount of air space contained in the pattern, can help you determine the visual weight of a design.

WILD ROSE

STRAWBERRY

The wild-rose design at top left also fills its given space, yet it seems simply to *be* within its area rather than *be contained* within the space as does the grape-leaf pattern. The wild-rose pattern is created with six units—five leaf groups and one cluster of flowers. Since the design units are small in area, each contains finer details than the grape leaves. The wild-rose pattern contains much more air space than the grape-leaf design—nearly one-half of the basic triangle shape is background work. Such a design would be considered a medium-weight enhancement.

The strawberry design at bottom left is a lightweight design. It seems to have little relationship to the space it occupies. The four units within the design—three leaves and one berry cluster—are seen quite separately as individual units, each self-contained. As with the wild rose, the small units will accept finer and lighter detailing. More than one-half of the triangle area is air space, and it is accented by the long, sweeping lines of the stems. Even the added strawberry runner floats on a cushion of air.

Implied Weight

Whereas the visual weight of the design is created by the artist, the implied weight is inferred by the viewer. The viewer uses that knowledge to judge the appropriateness of the design. The grape-leaf design represents one small part of the grapevine, a massive plant that can reach to the very canopy of the tree or trellis that it uses for its natural support. Eventually, the grapevine can overtake the trellis, and the base trunk of an old grapevine can easily reach 5 in. to 6 in. in width.

By contrast, the wild rose is a shrub that might reach 10 ft. to 12 ft. in height and up to 15 ft. in width. It has long, sweeping branches that arch down toward the ground. When in full bloom it seems almost to droop with the weight of its own flowers. What hardwood stems the wild rose has are hidden within the depths of the plant. This is a self-supporting plant, yet if grown in an upright position, it would need a trellis to hold its branches.

Finally, the strawberry is a perennial plant that reaches only 8 in. to 10 in. in height. Each year it dies back to the ground, preserving only a few leaves to begin its new growth in the spring. This plant is small and fragile in comparison to the grapevine or the wild rose.

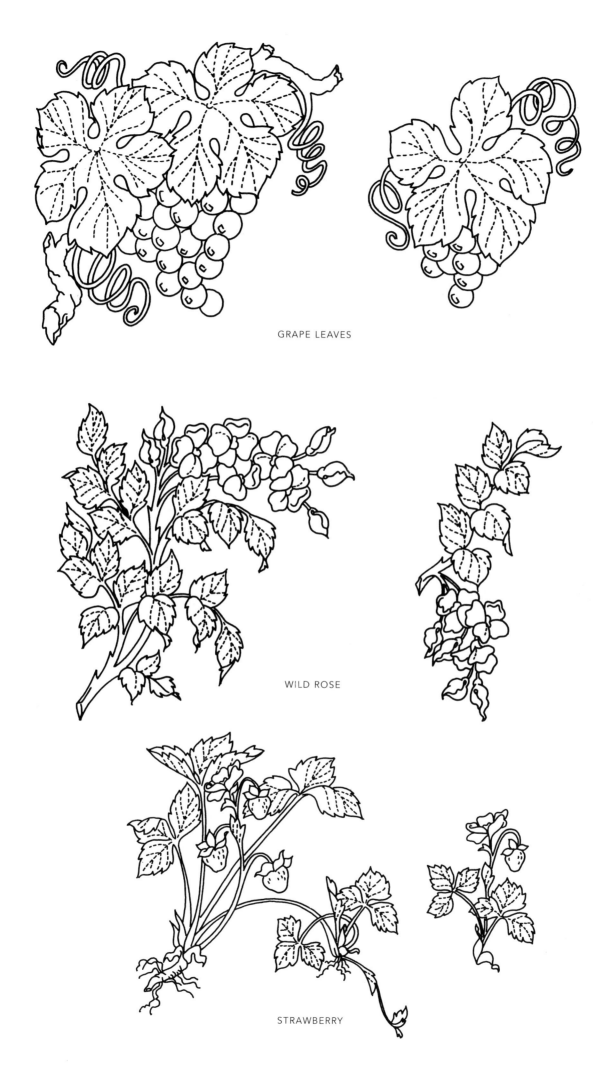

GRAPE LEAVES

WILD ROSE

STRAWBERRY

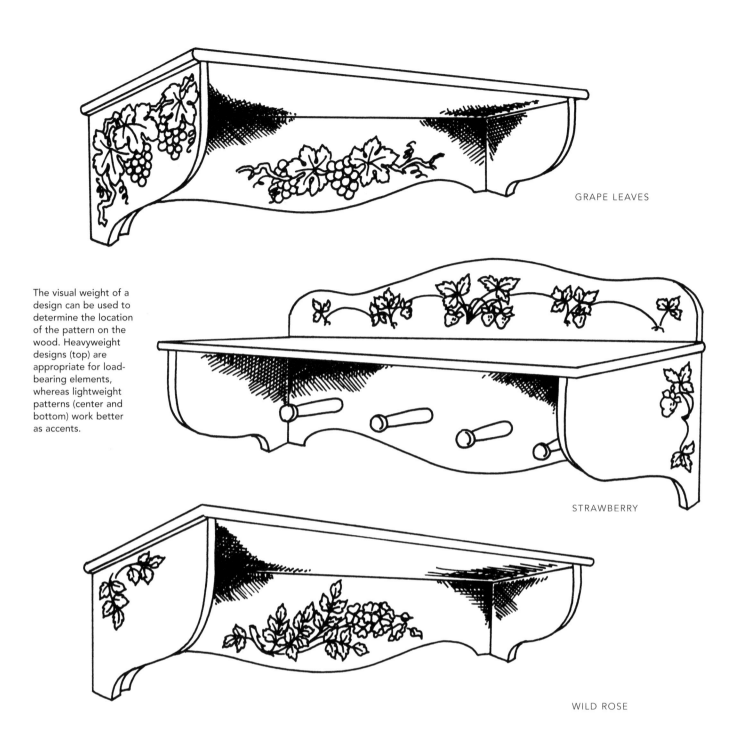

GRAPE LEAVES

The visual weight of a design can be used to determine the location of the pattern on the wood. Heavyweight designs (top) are appropriate for load-bearing elements, whereas lightweight patterns (center and bottom) work better as accents.

STRAWBERRY

WILD ROSE

When choosing which design to use on a wood element and where to use it, you need to balance the visual weight and the implied weight. On a simple wall-mounted bookshelf (see the drawings above), the grape-leaf design is visually strong enough and heavy enough to be used on the shelf supports. Just as the grapevine is strong enough to create its own trellis, its design will be strong enough to hold the weight of the books on the shelf.

The wild rose, though self-supporting, cannot support the weight of the books and should not be used on a main, load-bearing member of the shelf (except as a small accent). This design would be more appropriate on the lower back board, which adds stability to the form yet carries very little of the load of the shelf.

Finally, the small and fragile strawberry plant would be an excellent accent for an upper back board. Here it can reach for the air, resting on the shelf, without any weight from the books.

MARGINS AND AIR SPACE

Design work needs to fit the form on which it is used. If the pattern is too large or overworked, it will overpower the piece and make it appear heavy and visually oppressive (see the drawing at left above). If the pattern is too small and isolated, it can become lost and insignificant (see the drawing at right above). With the careful use of margins and air space throughout the design, both situations can easily be avoided.

When artists place a painting or a print in a frame, they often surround the artwork with a mat. The mat provides an air space or visual pause between the work created in the painting and the wood frame. The mat allows the viewer to explore the painting and then to place it within the boundaries of the frame; it unites the two individual elements that complete the final picture.

You can use this same principle when placing a pattern on a wooden form: Creating an air space between the design work and the edge of the element has the same effect as using a mat around an art print. By using a carefully measured distance between the edge of the wood and the edge of the pattern, you can create a visual margin that allows the viewer's eye to make the transition between the pattern and the form (see the drawing below). Repeating this visual margin wherever the pattern is used provides continuity throughout the final form of the furniture.

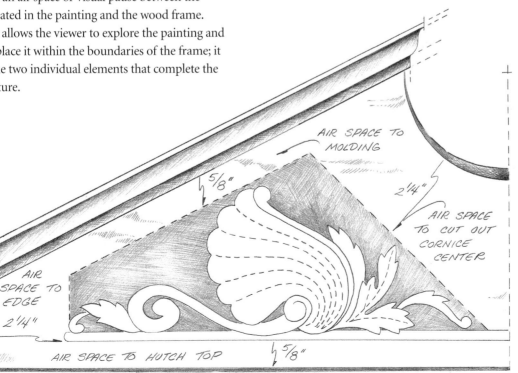

Allowing an equal margin at the top and bottom of the pattern and an equal margin at the sides centers the design within the space.

Different-shaped patterns require different treatment when sizing the design and the margin.

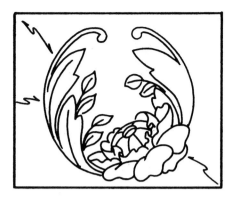

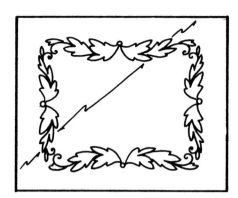

Make sure to choose a margin that is in proportion to the wood element on which it is used. As a general rule, I make the margins about one-eighth of the measurement of the wood element. For example, on a 16-in.-wide door panel I'd use margins about 2 in. wide around the outside edge, to give a pattern area approximately 12 in. wide.

Some patterns create their own margins and air space. Using a circular pattern on a square wood element automatically allows for uncarved or unpainted areas at each corner (as in the poppy circle in the drawing at top left). In this situation, you can bring a pattern close to the edges of the panel using a narrow margin along the sides. When using a square or rectangular pattern based on a linear design (see the drawing at top right), not only will there be margins around the outer edge but also air space within the design work. If you fill in the rectangular design with a quilting pattern (see the drawing at bottom left), the only air space for the design will be the margins that you allow. Mirror images and free-form designs tend to contain extra air space because they do not use controlled or static boundaries (see the drawing at bottom right).

The open areas and carved areas interblend within the pattern. With this style of pattern the margins are established from the individual units of the design.

If the margin around the pattern is more than one-third to one-half the width of the wood element, the design will be overpowered by the furniture. Consider enlarging the design to a more reasonable size, repeating the pattern in a mirror image to double its size, or adding a border or line accent to extend its given area. If, on the other hand, the pattern touches any edge of the wood element or seems to be crowded within the boundaries of the structure, you might wish to reduce the size of the pattern.

TESTING THE PATTERN

Just as "measure twice and cut once" is a fundamental rule for carpenters and cabinetmakers, "test the pattern before you begin" should be the watchword for all wood carvers, wood burners, and wood painters. Making a simple test pattern on paper of the completed piece of furniture with the pattern in position can save hours of needless correction work.

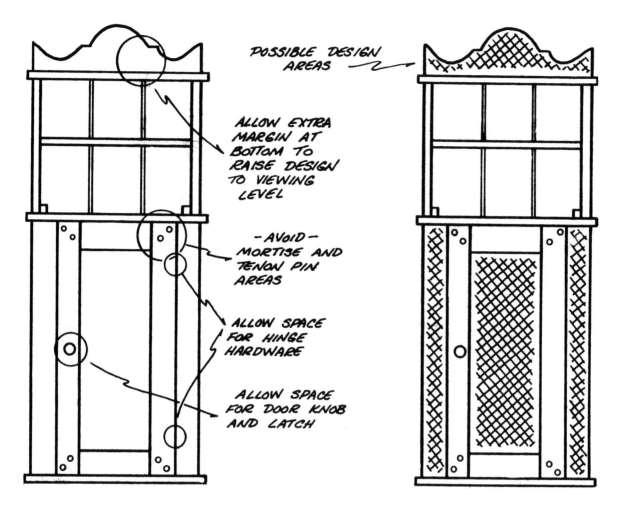

POSSIBLE DESIGN AREAS

ALLOW EXTRA MARGIN AT BOTTOM TO RAISE DESIGN TO VIEWING LEVEL

—AVOID—
MORTISE AND TENON PIN AREAS

ALLOW SPACE FOR HINGE HARDWARE

ALLOW SPACE FOR DOOR KNOB AND LATCH

Planning the location of the pattern work on the completed piece of furniture is a critical part of the design process.

When making a test pattern, keep both the wood form and the pattern in correct proportion to each other. Allow for all margins and air spaces that will be needed to fit the pattern to the piece (see the drawings above). Check the final test draft for continuity and for visual impact.

There are times when you may want to accent a wood form that has already been completed, as when you're adding a painted design to refinished furniture. In this case, sample patterns can be made and taped or tacked directly onto the piece before work begins. As with the test draft on paper, the pattern may then be viewed and any corrections in the design can be made before work begins. By using the test patterns, any changes that need to be made can be planned in advance.

As you work on the test pattern, keep in mind the following questions:

• What impacts the viewer first, the pattern and design work or the wood form of the furniture?

If the pattern work is prominent, scale it back to avoid overpowering the form. If, on the other hand, the pattern work is scattered in small, indistinct areas throughout the form, you may want to rework it so the designs do not become isolated on the piece.

• Does one area of the test draft seem heavier or lighter with pattern work than other areas?

For example, if there is a concentration of design work on the door panels of a hutch, it might be better balanced by adding a design to the drawers.

• Does the pattern work complement both the style of the furniture and its final use?

If the pattern is a traditional heavy-leaf pattern, it may not be appropriate for a country-style blanket chest. Conversely, a pattern design of country geese might be better replaced with a traditional scroll or shell for use on a glassware hutch in a formal dining room.

• Does the pattern work have the visual weight to support or accentuate its given wood element?

If the pattern is appropriate in size to the area but seems too heavy visually, it can overpower the element

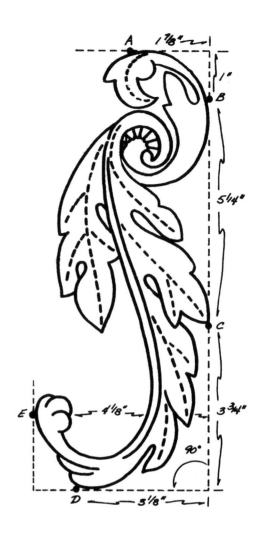

Once the test pattern has been completed on paper and any adjustments have been made, the design is ready to be transferred to the wood.

on which it is placed. If the pattern is appropriate in size but visually too light in weight, it can create a feeling that the design will be crushed by the wood form.

• Does the pattern work interfere with the final use of the wood form?

If the pattern extends from the back rail of a chair to its arm rests, the finished carving might be uncomfortable for the user. If the pattern extends to any edges, as along a drawer front, the work can easily be damaged with use.

• When the furniture is completed where will it most likely be displayed?

If in your original test plan you have included design work that will be hidden by a wall, such as carvings on the sides of a corner cupboard, this work will be lost when the piece is placed in its final position. If a desk will be freestanding in an office with a visitor's chair in front of it, the piece may need accent work on both the drawer side and on the back side so the carving can be seen both by the person sitting at the desk and by the visitor.

• Does the pattern work allow areas for any hardware that may be required on the furniture?

If a dresser drawer will require two drawer handles, you'll need to leave unaccented areas in the pattern for their placement.

• Does the pattern conflict with any features of the construction of the woodworking?

If the corners or edges of the form are constructed with decorative joinery techniques (such as dovetails), the pattern should not hide or disguise the work. If the pattern work does not allow enough margin or air space around the design, it may encroach upon edge details inherent in the form.

• Does the pattern invite the viewer to interact with the finished project.

If the pattern is well placed, it will focus the eye of the user on doors and drawers that ask to be opened. If the accents are well designed, they will encourage the user to touch the depths of the carving or feel the texture of the wood burning.

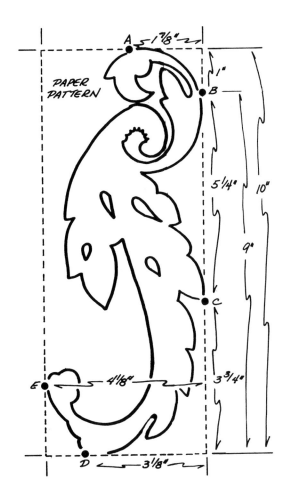

PAPER PATTERN

A ⟵ 1⅞" ⟶
B
1"
5¼" 10"
9"
C
3¾"
E ⟵ 4⅛" ⟶
D ⟵ 3⅛" ⟶

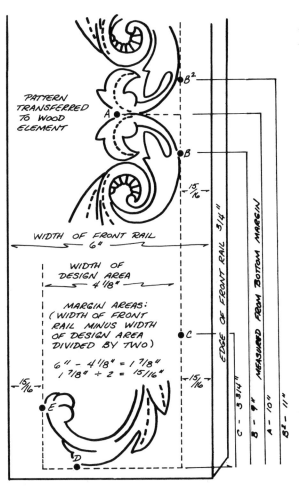

PATTERN TRANSFERRED TO WOOD ELEMENT

B²
A
B
15/16
WIDTH OF FRONT RAIL 6"
WIDTH OF DESIGN AREA 4⅛"
MARGIN AREAS:
(WIDTH OF FRONT RAIL MINUS WIDTH OF DESIGN AREA DIVIDED BY TWO)
6" − 4⅛" = 1⅞"
1⅞" ÷ 2 = 15/16"
15/16
C
15/16
EDGE OF FRONT RAIL 5¼"
MEASURED FROM BOTTOM MARGIN
C − 3¾"
B − 9"
A − 10"
B² − 11"
E
D

When transferring the pattern, all register marks and margin allowances are made on the paper pattern, and then repeated on the wood for accurate placement.

TRANSFERRING THE PATTERN TO PAPER

Once you've chosen and tested the design that you wish to carve, burn, or paint, you'll need to make a copy of the pattern on a sheet of paper. There are several ways to trace a pattern easily and accurately without damaging the original pattern.

The simplest way to copy a pattern is to use a sheet of tracing paper; tracing velum and "onion-skin" typing paper both work well. Use very light pressure on the tracing pencil. Pressing too heavily will leave an impression from the pencil point in the original design. If you use a marker to trace the pattern, first test the marker on the tracing paper to make sure that the ink will not bleed through onto the original.

The pattern that you have chosen will often be used several times on a piece of furniture, both as it was originally traced and as a reverse copy. Onion-skin typing paper, although excellent for lifting the pattern, does not survive repeated tracing without tearing along the pencil lines. You'll need to make a new copy onto heavier paper, or make several copies using the onion skin.

A quick and easy way to transfer a pattern to a new piece of paper is to tape the pattern to the glass of a sunny window. Place a sheet of paper over the pattern and tape it into place. The light coming through the window will allow you to clearly see and trace the design. To reverse the pattern, simply tape the original design to the window with the pattern facing away from you.

To turn a pattern into a mirror image, trace the pattern onto one-half of a large sheet of paper. Fold the paper in half so that the fold line falls along what will become the centerline of the mirror image. Place the design with the sketch against the window and the clean half of the paper facing you. When you have traced the design and opened the paper, the sketch work and the tracing will be opposing, aligned, and ready for use. Symmetrical designs are more accurately created by sketching one-half of the pattern and then tracing the second half in reverse.

Another way to transfer the pattern is to use a light-box. You can make a lightbox with a piece of safety glass, several books, and a clip-on light or flashlight. Prop the back end of the glass evenly on two stacks of books to raise it 4 in. or 5 in. off the table. Place the light, facing toward the front edge of the glass, between the book stacks (see the drawing below). Turn off the room lights. Put the original pattern on top of the glass and cover it with a clean sheet of paper. The light from the clip-on light, just as the light from a sunny window, will allow you to see the pattern lines and make it easy to trace a copy onto the new sheet of paper.

Once you have experienced the convenience of using a lightbox, you may wish to add one to your design equipment. Lightboxes in various sizes, from desk models to freestanding table models, can be purchased through art-supply catalogs and office-supply stores. You can also make your own lightbox in your wood-shop using lamp parts that are available in woodworking catalogs and glass that can be purchased at your local hardware store.

It often happens that the pattern you wish to use does not fit the shape of your workpiece. For example, you may be looking for a corner pattern but the design you like is a straight line. The solution is to modify the pattern to fit your work. Make several copies of the pattern and then cut the design into small units: groups of leaves, clusters of flowers, and segments of ribbon or scrollwork. These smaller groups can then be arranged into the shape of your work, taped into their final position, and retraced to create your own arrangement (see the drawing on the facing page).

If the pattern you want to use is too small or too big, you can enlarge or reduce it on a photocopying machine. Using photocopies allows you to try several different sizes of the pattern without having to spend hours redrawing the pattern yourself. You can also use a pantograph to reproduce a design in any size. This simple device can be found for sale in many wood-working catalogs and is a wonderful addition to your design equipment.

TRANSFERRING THE PATTERN TO WOOD

Once the pattern has been traced onto working sheets of paper, you are ready to transfer it to the wood. The easiest way to transfer the design is to use typing carbon paper, which leaves a clean dark line that will not accidentally rub off. Working with carbon paper is an effective method when you are making only a few copies of the design, but the carbon paper will not with-stand repeated use without tearing. When using carbon paper, be careful to trace as accurately as possible, since the lines can only be removed from the wood complete-ly either by carving or by sanding them out.

A second quick way to trace the pattern onto wood is to blacken the back of the pattern paper with a soft lead pencil. Be sure to cover the area completely with the pencil. Now position the pattern with the black-ened surface against the wood and trace over the design. As with carbon paper, this method is only good for a few copies before the pattern paper becomes too worn. However, it does avoid the problem of

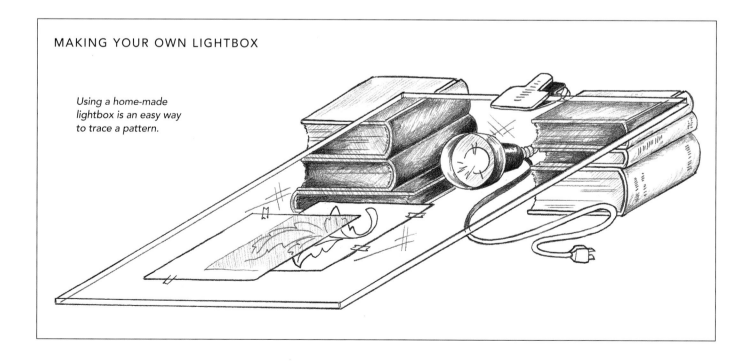

MAKING YOUR OWN LIGHTBOX

Using a home-made lightbox is an easy way to trace a pattern.

MODIFYING A PATTERN

You can create your own pattern or adjust the shape of an existing pattern by making several copies of different designs, cutting them apart, and then rearranging them into a new design.

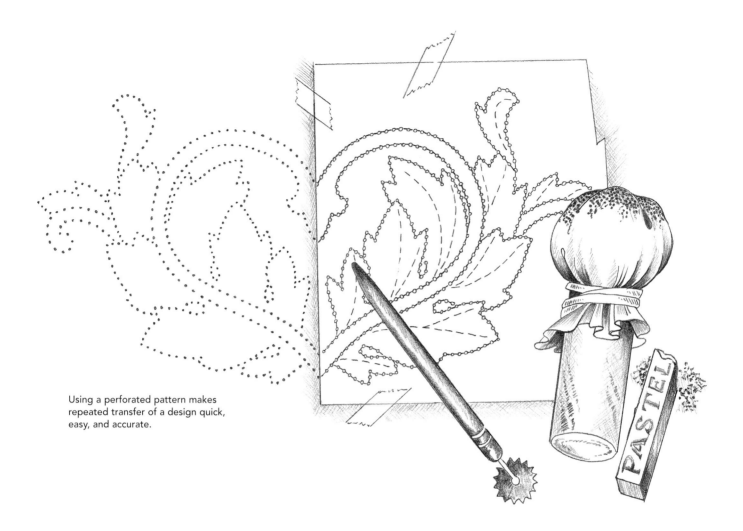

Using a perforated pattern makes repeated transfer of a design quick, easy, and accurate.

working with layers of paper, and the pencil marks that are made on the wood can be removed with an eraser. Once the pattern has been transferred, the pencil lines on the wood can be darkened by going over them again with the pencil.

When working on a dark-colored surface, regular carbon-paper tracing lines may not show well enough to work with easily. You can buy colored carbon paper from sewing stores and fabric shops, or rub white chalk across a rough-toothed paper to make an excellent tracing paper with light-colored lines.

To transfer large patterns to wood, metal, or painted surfaces, use sheets of newspaper instead of carbon paper. The newsprint ink will become a finely dotted line from which you can work. Any newsprint that is left after the work has been completed may be removed with a pencil eraser on wood or with a window-cleaner solution on painted and metal surfaces.

If you intend to use the same design over and over again, consider making a perforated pattern to save time over hand tracing (see the drawing above). Place the pattern to be used over a thick layer of newspaper.

Using a tracing wheel (available from fabric stores), firmly and slowly roll over all of the design lines. Lightly sand the back of the pattern paper with fine sandpaper to open all of the holes. Tape the pattern into place on the project and dust lightly with carbon dust for a dark tracing line or with chalk or talcum powder for a light-colored line.

With patterns that you know you'll use again and again, another way to save time is to make a template out of lightweight cardboard. Trace the pattern onto the cardboard, and then cut it out (use an X-acto knife to cut the inside lines). To use the template, place it on the workpiece and glide a pencil around the outside edge and through the inside cutouts. To keep the template from sliding, glue a piece of fine sandpaper to the template on the side of the design that will contact the work.

Sources for Design Ideas

The patterns presented in this book should give you enough ideas to keep you carving, burning, or painting for many years to come. But if you're looking for new ideas, you might consider lifting designs from antique furniture, old gravestones, or even wallpaper.

Taking a pencil rubbing of carved relief work on furniture and gravestones is a good way to lift an intricate design.

Lifting a design from an antique piece of furniture can be difficult since you don't want to damage or mark the wood during the tracing process. To protect the piece, tape the pattern paper over the design work and use the flat edge of a soft pencil to cover the paper with graphite. As the pencil flat hits an edge of the design it will leave a darker mark (see the drawing above). The darker lines on the pattern paper can then be transferred to a new sheet of paper.

Sometimes the design that you wish to copy is too deeply carved to lift with a graphite rubbing. In this case, try taping a sheet of stiff tracing paper over the work. Use your finger to press the paper into the carving, causing the paper to crinkle and crease. The lines created by this pressing process will become your pattern.

Many old gravestones from the 1700s and 1800s have beautifully carved relief designs. To lift a design from a gravestone, you'll need a sheet of lightweight paper that completely covers the stone, a dabbing stick, and some carbon dust. To make a dabbing stick, first cover one end of a short piece of 1-in. dowel with a large wrap of cotton. Then place a piece of soft fabric, such

as T-shirt material, over the cotton wrap and secure it to the dowel with cord or rubber bands (see the drawing on the facing page). This will create a firm cotton-stuffed ball of fabric with a handle. Carbon dust can be obtained at an art-supply store, or you can make your own rubbing dust by grinding up soft pastel sticks. With the lightweight paper secured to the stone, pat the dabbing stick with dust, gently tap off any excess, and then rub the cotton-ball area over the design on the stone. Just as the flat of the pencil will leave darker marks on the paper where it contacts the relief, so will the rubbing dust. Work from the top of the stone down so that the excess dust does not obscure your work.

There are many other sources for design ideas. Wall-paper and fabric prints offer ideas on small repetitive patterns. Children's coloring books are a good source for simple shapes and childhood themes. Books on classic architecture provide ideas for corner patterns, panel designs, and scrollwork. Keep a file of any designs that catch your interest, and you'll have a ready reference at your fingertips as you plan new work.

INDEX OF PATTERNS

PUBLISHER
James P. Chiavelli

ACQUISITIONS EDITOR
Rick Peters

PUBLISHING COORDINATOR
Joanne Renna

EDITOR
Peter Chapman

DESIGNER/LAYOUT ARTIST
Carol Singer

PHOTOGRAPHERS
Boyd Hagen (*pgs. 1, 170*)
Scott Phillips (*all others*)

TYPEFACE
Minion

PAPER
70-lb. Patina Matte

PRINTER
R.R. Donnelley, Willard, Ohio

TRICIA GUILD
PAINT BOX

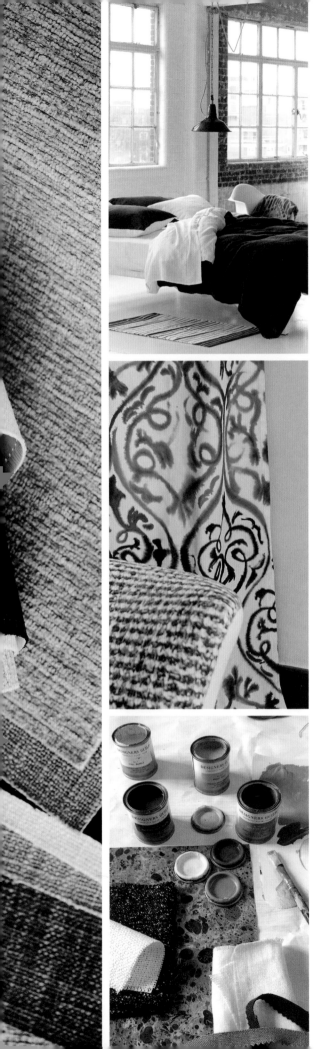

TRICIA GUILD
PAINT BOX

**45 PALETTES FOR CHOOSING
COLOR, TEXTURE AND PATTERN**

photography by James Merrell
text by Tricia Guild with Amanda Back

quadrille

For my brilliant team—
Amanda, Jo and Meryl

Palette directory

This book contains 45 unique palettes, each featuring a strip of colors. Details of matching Designers Guild paints, wallpapers or fabrics for all the colors can be found on pages 182–5

Mood boards

Details of the Designers Guild paints, wallpapers and fabrics featured in the mood boards in the book are shown on pages 186–9

Mood board see page 186

contents

foreword

When I consider some of my favorite artists whose work has particularly touched me, it is inevitably their sense of color that I find intriguing and memorable. This is an instinctive, primal reaction, a response that comes from the soul and stays with you. Color has this power: to evoke an emotion, change a mood, uplift your spirits and make life feel better.

Over the years I have met many people who are more than a little nervous of embracing color in their own homes. There is a reticence and anxiety that prevents them from choosing anything that might be considered a little daring or even expressive. At Designers Guild, it has always been our passionate goal to give people the confidence to live with the colors and textures that we know will simply enrich their lives. Our aim is to share that sense of unadulterated joy one feels when contemplating a glorious landscape or perhaps a work of art that touches you deeply. To imbue one's home with the same expression and personality is to harness the power of color in your own way. It is a quest that will always excite and energize me.

On the following pages I would like to share with you the way I choose colors I love, put them together in a palette, then use this in a mix of plains, pattern and texture to evoke the mood I seek in a room. This is an approach I feel we can all use in our homes and I wish you joy in experimenting with it. All you need to do now is open your own paint box and get creative!

Tricia Guild

In this book I hope to demystify the process of decorating with the colors you love; to inspire you to find your own sense of color and discover just how enjoyable it can be to put it into practice.

creating a palette

Working with color, pattern and texture to create exciting new ideas for our homes is my lifelong passion as well as my job. I have a rather instinctive approach to color and the collections of fabrics, wallpapers, paints and accessories that I create and use are in many ways my own artist's palette.

In this book I have lifted the lid on my own "paint box"—the colors with which I choose to color my world. I have collated some of my favorite palettes, inspired by nature, my travels, art and architecture, fashion and the everyday combinations of colors that surround us. They can all be adapted to suit your style and your home and, although many may feature pattern, every single one will work like a dream in purely plain colors. Here are a few pointers to get you going:

Feel it "Where do I start?" is a familiar refrain when approaching the decoration of a room. I suggest that a good place to start is to consider how you want your home to feel, or rather, how you want to feel when you are in it. Are you after cosseting, cosy comfort or slick, stylish practicality? Do you prefer a classical space or a contemporary one? The energy in our homes comes largely from the way we live in them, so make this the first box to tick.

Live it Consider the function of the space: will you be entertaining regularly here or should it have a quieter feel? Is this a place to display art or a collection of some sort, or are you after a calm retreat? A family room or a room of one's own? The function of your space will dictate its flow and how you choose to live in it.

Gather it Research ideas and the styles that you love: trawl through magazines, visit museums and art galleries, films and theatre, collect postcards from your travels, scour the internet and gather your ideas together to hone your own style. Be inspired!

Accommodate it Not many of us start with a blank canvas, so bear in mind any architectural features, pieces of furniture and other possessions that will be in the room. Their colors and textures will affect your choice of palette and how you balance it in the space.

Light it Consider the natural light entering the room, or the lighting you plan to install. Both will have a significant effect on the way color is represented and therefore how the space feels. But of course both light and shades or tones of color can be manipulated and altered to suit the mood.

Pull it together All the factors above will have a bearing on the colors and palette you choose to live with and it is bringing them all together which causes many to stumble. However, creating your own special palette, your own language of colors to express yourself, will be one of the most fulfilling aspects of decorating your home.

Color it There are a few key points to consider before you finalize your palette:

■ Identify the main colors that you love: are they cool or warm? Your main colors will dictate the type of white or neutral that you will undoubtedly need.

■ Balance tone and shade: Mixing a color with a neutral such as black, white or gray reduces the

colorfulness and alters the tone or the shade. Technically, a shade is a color with black added and is therefore darker than the original color; a tone is produced by adding gray and is softer than the original color. In practice, however, tones and shades are much more subtle, created not just with the addition of neutrals. For instance, we have many different whites in our collection, created by adding blue, red or yellow amongst other colors. It is the underlying tone of these colors that subtly delivers a force all of its own. It is important to understand the subtlety of underlying tones so that you can employ them effectively.

Imagine turning up the volume on a color, or for that matter turning it down. When you do this, you essentially find shades of the same color. Using multiple shades of one color is a harmonious way of breaking up a palette without veering too drastically from the path. For example, you may use a calm battleship gray as your main decorating color, with a much lighter shade on furniture and a darker shade on woodwork. Although the overall effect will be three different colors, they are derived from each other and are thus harmonious.

■ Find your neutral: A neutral is the color that underpins your scheme, providing a constant harmonious note. White is very often the default option, but why not consider one of these more interesting choices: it could be gray, ecru, chocolate, a shade of blue or green, or even pale plaster pink. I often use a shade of slate blue as a neutral, especially with bright colors, which allows the strong colors to sing but also stands up to them; or an olive green, which echoes the green in a garden.

More often than not white will feature as the neutral in your palette, in which case it is vital that your white complements the other colors or it will upset the balance of your space. For example, if you are using a rich cobalt blue your room will demand a clear blue-based white to complement it—a yellow-based white would look dirty next to the blue and a red-toned white would clash. In general, the following applies: a blue-based white will feel crisp and cool; a yellow-based white will feel more classical and warm; a red-based white works well with warmer tones and feels harmonious.

■ Add an accent: sometimes you might choose a simple palette of one or two colors, but often you will want to use more, so an accent color can play a useful role, especially if you would like to add detail and definition, a jolt of energy and dynamism, or perhaps just an understated point of contrast.

Get creative A great way to assess if your ideas will actually work is to create a mood board, an excellent way of judging the relationship between the different elements you plan to use in a room and seeing if they work. When making your mood board, the trick is to use each color/pattern/element at the same scale as it will be used in the room: if you have a large wall of blue and a small window of green ensure the two colors are represented at the correct scale on the mood board. If it works on paper, it will work in your home. We have shown mood boards for some of the palettes in this book. For details please see pages 186–9.

If you still feel nervous about creating your own palette why not choose one from the following pages. Each palette tells a story, of its inspiration and how it is created, with advice on how to use it. The strip of colors down the side gives you options for colors that will all work well together—you can choose the ones you prefer for your own scheme. And all the colors are cross-referenced to Designers Guild paints, wallpapers and fabrics on pages 182–5.

I truly hope you enjoy working with this book and that it gives you the confidence to find your own sense of style and color.

Mood board see page 186

white
on white

In many ways there can be no better starting point than decorating with white. White is vital: it is one of the building blocks of any scheme and as an auxiliary color it is extraordinarily important — it adds lightness and modernity, crisp graphic detailing and airy expanse to vivid strong color or pattern. However, to assume that because we use it more than any other color it must be easy would be to make a common but potentially damning mistake. The many different shades of white can clash, so a mix of the wrong whites can look, at best, cold and dull; at worst, slightly dirty and sad. Decorating a room that is all white can be one of the most difficult schemes to pull off. It really should be approached with the same caution as if one were decorating with seemingly more challenging colors. The first thing to determine is, which white are you? Which white is going to work best in your space and bounce the light effectively? A blue-toned white will work well in sunny light-filled rooms; a creamy yellow-toned white will feel more classical and perfectly suit a colder-feeling or north-facing space; a gray-toned white will give you a clear, crisp architectural finish. Living with white can be magical, so long as you approach it with vigor and it is a determined choice.

■ When choosing an all-white room ensure that all aspects — walls, drapes, shades, furniture, accessories etc — are united in their tones of white, to avoid potential pitfalls.

14

15

During the seventeenth century the Dutch East India Company began bringing back examples of the finest Chinese porcelain. Refined and elegant, with layers of blue-and-white pattern, it was immediately much in demand. Soon, the potters of Delft were creating their own pieces, inspired by the colors of Chinese porcelain but using local materials and their own culture as subject matter. Delft blue-and-white tiles became famous for their simplicity and evocative nature and have, over the centuries, adorned every possible kind of interior from humble homes to some of the finest royal palaces in the world, their particular kind of classlessness and spirit equally at home in both.

In the intervening years the marriage of blue and white has become one of the most popular palettes in the world. As more natural pigments and then synthetic compounds became available many new shades of both blue and white were utilized and combined, leading to variations on this palette appearing all over Europe, in America and the Far East. The very names of the individual blues—indigo, lapis, midnight, cobalt, cornflower, azure, Prussian blue—evoke a wide variety of sources, inspiration and moods. White, too, has many shades to choose from.

This classic combination relies heavily on its simplicity—dreamy, egalitarian, workaday, almost like a uniform—but despite its simple appearance one must still take care to create the necessary harmony and balance for it to succeed. The exact tones of blue and white are crucial; both elements should come from the same tonal family for the palette to work.

classic blue and white

- A warm blue and white feels traditional and offers a comforting and gentle spirit. A cooler hued combination, on the other hand, will feel crisp and modern.

- Use the darkest form of your chosen blue to add definition and, by using derivatives of this strong color throughout the room, you will ensure continuity and harmony throughout.

- This palette does not really need any shouts of contrast, but further interest and depth can be created with different textures. For example, mix linen with silk and wool or velvet—contrasting textures that are united by the simplicity of these two colors.

- As seen on the following pages, varying the mix of patterns and plains on walls, windows and fabrics will also change the mood of this versatile palette.

Keep the palette tightly controlled and allow pattern and textures to create the energy and dynamism in your space.

light white Here, white is the dominant color, emphasizing the high ceilings and spaciousness, while rich
tones of indigo, navy, cobalt and Prussian blue mix with dashes of kingfisher blue to bring a feeling
of sophisticated intimacy to the seating area. Velvets, tweeds and sturdy linens work off one another
and add a vital mix of texture while pattern is kept small scale, geometric and tailored.
The result is a sleek and contemporary incarnation of a palette that is seemingly classic.

In this striking open space the combination of blue and white shows a different personality from the patterned blue on white of the previous pages.

The majestic heights of Mount Fuji rise from a plateau around 60 miles south west of Tokyo on Japan's Honshu Island. It is Japan's highest mountain and for centuries its perfectly symmetrical, snow-capped form has enjoyed huge cultural and spiritual symbolism. It has inspired poetry, prose and countless works of art, none more famous than that of the nineteenth-century artist Katsushika Hokusai. His iconic work—*Thirty-six Views of Mount Fuji*—is an extraordinary testament not only to the mountain's captivating beauty but to the glorious art form that is Japanese woodblock printing. In this hauntingly beautiful series of works, the artist made particular use of a very specific and, at the time, new blue known as Prussian or Berlin Blue, the first modern chemical pigment. This new color enabled Hokusai to detail the depth of water and recreate the intensity of the landscape, be it lakes, skies and mountains or temples, bridges and boats. In his iconic work, Prussian blue is used as a base in a palette that is both serene and timeless yet with an evocative character. The works are highlighted with jade, white and turquoise and defined with the charcoal tones of Sumi black—the particular ink of the Japanese wood block artist. All are exquisite in their detailing.

This palette pays homage to Hokusai's work. It is extremely easy to live with, its cool softness evoking a feeling of quiet calm. Cool and warm blues are mixed to great effect: cool sky-blue, moonstone and turquoise are enriched by warm and dynamic Prussian blue and cobalt. The combination is perfectly balanced by a soft dove gray that forms the neutral

Mount Fuji views

base, allowing the other blue shades to soar. In this particular room, a lively mix of textures adds another layer of interest: printed velvets mix with plain and sturdy striped linens while a large-scale wallpaper panel sets the tone. A sharp, brilliant white adds contrast and freshness while Sumi ink black defines the mix and gives it a graphic edge.

- The balance between warm and cool is crucial here so identify your perfect pale gray first. If you then want to add more colors to this base stay tonal and go for jade green, turquoise or denim.

- Don't forget that textures are part of the language of your room and you can change them to manipulate the scheme. For example a shimmering silk will feel glamorous, whereas a robust and hard-wearing linen less so.

23

Powerful and earthy: indigo mixed with cornflower and cobalt is as elegant as it is timeless.

silk road blues

Indigo blue, a deep, powerful color, is as resonant and timeless as the earth itself. Taking its name from the indigofera plant, whose leaves were picked and carefully fermented to create the dye that gives us this ubiquitous color, it has a rich intensity and mystery that brings to mind moonlit skies and the inky dramatic darkness of desert nights. First produced in India and eastern Asia, indigo proceeded to link the world via the Silk Route, along which for centuries it was traded and bartered, replacing woad as the dark blue dye of choice and prized for its extraordinarily rich tones. Yet as ancient as it may be, its relevance to contemporary culture is undisputed. Its best-known use today is as the color of our modern-day uniform of choice—the humble pair of jeans. The sixth color of the rainbow and part of the color spectrum, it exerts its influence with authority and strength, refuting the very idea that blue is cold with its obvious warmth.

In this palette, the dark yet serene tones of indigo are partnered with cornflower, cobalt, delft and turquoise as well as a pale washed natural linen and a soft chalky tone of white. It is an earthy group of colors, each taken from nature itself and as softly tonal as a watercolor seascape wash on thick creamy paper. Used in this way, without any jarring notes of contrast or sharp punches of accent color, these warm tones of blue exude calm, down-to-earth simplicity and a serenity that invites you to relax and unwind. The palette represents an effortless and nonchalant chic that is at the same time striking in its assuredness. It is as though it is entirely comfortable in its relaxed vibe and has nothing to prove to anyone.

Scandinavian cool

I am constantly inspired by the relaxed and effortless cool of Scandinavia. Here, the northern landscape seems to take centre stage: the forests of pine, wildflower meadows, fjords, lakes and archipelagos of tiny islands that define the topography of these nations all contribute to their inherent and restrained sense of style.

This palette demonstrates how indigo, star of the previous palette, can be used in an informal way in a light-filled contemporary space. Here, a faded denim blue is paired with soft chalky white, fern green, slate blue and lead-pencil gray. There is a natural coolness to the palette yet it does not feel cold: the mellow blue is calm and reflective, a perfect fit with its white partner. A more vivid leafy green adds its unique dose of vitality, while the lead gray details and defines with a serene touch.

- The more white you use, the lighter and brighter your space will feel. For a slightly richer feeling, use more lead gray as a neutral, keeping white more to the sidelines.

- As the palette is quite tight, with only green as an accent, you can mix colors and textures easily if you stick to your chosen colors.

The endless, dizzying expanse of blue that is a summer sky, lit by glorious sunshine, tempered only by the occasional fluffy cloud— there is almost no color or sight more uplifting. This palette uses that midsummer blue as its base, adding vibrant shades of clematis pink, leaf green, citrine yellow and ubiquitous white to create a joyous combination, reminiscent of a summer garden, full of hope and optimism.

Just as in a garden, the definition in this palette really comes in the form of the warm yet lively leaf green. Without dominating, it links the rich pink, lemon yellow and chalky white with its sky-blue base as effortlessly as entwining strands of clematis. The rich green gray gives the palette an earthiness that magically grounds the singing clarity of the other tones. There are no sharp contrasts here or jolts of strong color; instead, evocative and soft accent colors that one can play with, increasing or decreasing their intensity to add a different element or change the mood. Despite its obvious summery feel, this scheme is not just suited to light-filled airy rooms; it works beautifully in darker, smaller spaces too.

mid-summer skies

- Intensify the tone of the palette to create a richer feeling: this works brilliantly in small rooms where deeper tones actually work best.

- In a sun-drenched light-filled room increase the white to add crispness. Conversely, in a darker room use more of the battleship gray for a softer feel.

- The tonality of the palette is its beauty, so to keep the feeling serene and soft use your chosen neutral plus one or two of your accent colors in accessories. Don't be tempted to use all the accent colors together.

- Use different textures to counteract any feeling of coldness in a room: wallpaper, velvet, wool, flannel and bouclé will all add a layer of richness and warmth, whatever palette you use.

cool summery shades

In this wonderfully light and open sitting room, the palette is used to great effect. Here the clear-toned dove gray provides a classic neutral backdrop with just enough gravity and warmth to add depth to the scheme and allow the brighter colors to sing. Leafy arrangements in simple vases pick out the green of the palette and echo the greens from the garden beyond.

A vibrant palette
straight out of a
mid-summer garden
infuses this room
with a lively
elegance. Crisp
white adds clarity
and modernity.

winter landscape

In winter there is a crisp coolness to our skies, when the sun is low and its light suffuses the landscape with a milky glow rather than the full-beam, intense bright light of summer. There is something magical and mysterious about winter, a season that signifies dormancy and finality. Yet there are still extraordinary colors to be found in this softly sleeping world. In northern climes, frost, snow and ice throw a glittering, white blanket over all below, creating an atmosphere of reflective calm —a still serenity that encourages us to slow down and stop.

There are times when a cool, wintry blast of ice blue is exactly what is needed, whatever the season. Cool colors need not actually feel cold; the trick is to evoke that feeling of calm mystery, stillness and reflection. This palette is a purposeful and refreshing example of cool blue at its best. The dominant color is a chalky, ice blue that is fresh, restrained and undeniably cool.

It is used alongside a pale green and a crisp, sharp white. The green is a crucial element —it feels lively and vital, and perfectly balances the blue. This cool trio of blue, white and green induce an overall sense of lightness and airiness. A soft blossom pink adds a note of warmth and femininity that just stops the palette from being too cold, while a surprising element of rich graphite adds definition, strength and modernity.

- This palette is designed to be used in rooms that are flooded with light, that therefore can take cooler colors; but if you love this mix it can easily be manipulated by using warm-toned versions of these colors.

- Add a richer tone of pink for a more feminine feeling.

- As always, the right white can make or break this palette—make sure your white has a blue or gray undertone to maintain that cool luminous feeling.

a sweep of ice-cool blue

In this stylish morning room the palette conveys its sense of mystery, calm and evocative stillness with aplomb. Notice the way the touches of pink add richness and warmth, with even the flowers adding their own energy to the space. White flowers or even green leaves will change the feel of a room, so use these changeable elements to reflect your mood.

Maiolica is the name given to a form of pottery developed in fifteenth-century Italy, when a group of potters started to use tin as a component in glazing their work. The effect of tin glazing was to provide a bright white opaque surface on which the vibrant colors of their painted patterns simply glowed.

It is the joyful intensity of pattern and color from those early Maiolica pieces that inspires this palette of rich cobalt, ultramarine and bright white with accents of soft yellow. The mix is given a flash of energy and modernity with a vivid rich red that, in a stroke, adds heat as well as dynamism.

This confident and exuberant palette can work brilliantly in any space: the base of blues is rich and warm, and can be manipulated to add more strength and punch or less as is desired. As with the Midsummer Skies palette on page 30 there is an inherent joyfulness and optimism, but here the gentle, whimsical nature is replaced with confidence and a sense of power.

Identifying the family of blues is very important and its success depends on the correct balance of power and strength. Whilst there are plenty of contrasting colors, they are perfectly balanced, with each one playing its part. The deepest tone of Prussian blue adds definition, while a soft china blue is a beautiful base on which to add more detail and depth.

maiolica

A sharp, clear white cuts through the richness, providing space and lightness that feel fresh and modern.

In this room, the palette is contained in the wallpaper: colors are lifted out and used as counterpoints around the room, each one dancing off the other in a variety of textures, patterns and plains. Harmony comes from the close-knit teamwork of the palette that, however strong, allows for a joyful and energetic vivaciousness.

- This palette is full of contrasts and one could add further richness with different textures and patterns.

- More rich red will add yet more femininity and warmth, but be sure to balance with white to keep the scheme fresh; otherwise it could appear heavy and cloying.

- For a lighter, more classical feel, pick out the soft primrose yellow and use as an accent.

balancing bold colors with white

As always, the use of white is critical: in this room a clean-lined, crisp white sofa adds modernity and space to the palette which is contained in the highly decorated walls. This large white expanse allows the pattern and the palette to sing and balances the richness perfectly.

Mood board see page 187 45

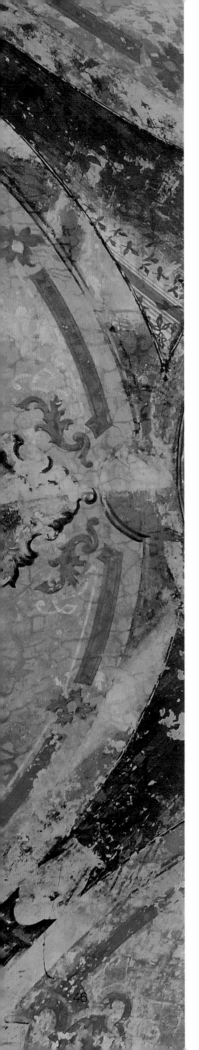

faded frescoes

I find medieval and Renaissance frescoes enchanting and, in particular, the works of the Italian artists Giotto and Perugino. I visit them regularly, always discovering something different, and they never fail to uplift and inspire with their extraordinary colors and details. The skillful technique of laying color and painting onto wet or fresh plaster has been practised and refined for centuries, the results giving the finished pieces of art a luminous and ethereal quality—almost as though there is a light source within. Over time, although the color softens, the frescoes retain their plastery undertones and sparkling tints.

This palette has been inspired by those now faded frescoes of Tuscany and Umbria that I love so much; clear, almost iridescent colors of lapis, azurite and ultramarine, viridian and amethyst have a lightness of touch that is rich yet easy to live with. They in turn are inspired by the landscape that surrounded the artists, as well as the sacred and classical themes they painted, so there is a timeless tranquillity that pervades the palette. A natural linen shade is the perfect foil for these cool tones, adding a soft warmth that balances the mix. These colors are linked by a clarity of tone that enables them to be used in any situation and the overriding mood is one of elegance and serenity.

- No need for hard strokes of definition in this palette. Simply use the deepest shades of the palette to add detail.

- Avoid any sharp blue-whites or gray-whites that would be too cold—keep your neutral soft and gentle to echo fresh or wet plaster.

- Against the faded washes of color on the walls patterned fabric can be used to add vitality and strength.

- One can alter the mood by employing pattern to add vitality and strength. Patterned wallpapers or fabrics retain the feeling of elegance but also feel more relaxed, whilst adding another dimension to your room.

Persian minakari

Minakari, the intricate art of enamelling, is a form of coloring and embellishing the surface of metals, tiles and jewelry by fusing over them vibrant colors in complex and often vivid designs. First recorded in Isfahan, Persia, over 1200 years ago, this beautiful decorative art form was exported to India and other countries by the Moguls in their conquests. Also known as the miniature of fire, it takes its name from the Persian word *mina*, meaning the azure of heaven, and makes abundant use of vivid hues of azure and cobalt blue, emerald green, scarlet and yellow.

This palette takes its cue from that rich heritage. Vibrant cobalt, ultramarine, turquoise and a lively emerald green are a dynamic and confident mix, tempered and balanced by a cool neutral stone. Although it may appear that the colors are from the cool side of the spectrum, their inherent richness and strength will lend a space warmth and intensity. A stroke of graphic charcoal could be a nod to the enameller's stylus, but adds a note of simplicity, too—slicing through the power of the palette and defining details, its strength an obvious and equal match to the force of the other tones. This particular room has plenty of light, but in a darker room the same palette could be employed just as effectively.

- For this palette to work, one needs to be confident. Success depends on the equal intensity of the corresponding tones of blue and green. They should be pure toned to stand up to each other and provide the dynamic strength.

- If you prefer a more classical look, keep your neutral warm. Alternatively if you want a more modern feel, and the light and architecture allow, adopt a cooler gray or off-white.

- A shocking pink could work as a contrast here—but just a shot: too much and you will lose the classicism of the palette.

Jewel bright tones of sapphire, emerald and amethyst inject a note of vivid dynamism and are as contemporary as they are timeless.

Swedish Gustavian

Whether you consider yourself a traditionalist or a modernist, urban or a lover of country style, there is something about a palette of chalky grays that seems to transcend any style, yet manages to work with them all. These particular soft shades of gray were used extensively in the palaces of King Gustav III of Sweden in the eighteenth century. They have become synonymous with a timeless grace and elegance that places equal billing on grandeur and ease. In this particular mix, the powdery grays form the backbone of the scheme. Other color is added with shades of celadon, duck egg, white pepper and white, while definition comes in the form not of gray, charcoal or black but instead a rich warm green. It is a restful and serene mix of gentle colors that feels soft and inviting. In this elegant suite of rooms the palette works beautifully, the doors, wood panelling and wooden furniture within featuring the pale pepper and cloudy gray that adds structure and continuity, whilst the whole palette is used on the walls in a wallpaper of gently trailing leaves and flowers, its own rather hypnotic rhythm adding to the charm and elegance of the rooms. The pattern is repeated as drapes at the window of the room beyond, a trick that links the two rooms effortlessly, adding a natural flow. The colors in this palette have been selected with a rich base note to warm up the cold northern light that floods the rooms. The color scheme is adhered to meticulously, which gives the room structure without appearing hard or overly formal.

The textures, too, are soft and natural: plaster-like walls, natural linen and soft velvet all add to the feeling of grace and informal elegance. The only accent in the rooms comes from white— there is no pop of color or jolt of contrast to steal the show, but rather a harmonious, tonal sense of ease that perfectly captures the sense of faded grandeur.

■ Using the soft pale gray is crucial as it is this that gives the room an anchor, while keeping the palette strict is also a clever trick; it lends a uniformity rather than formal structure.

■ These rooms do benefit from lots of light, albeit a cold northern light, so the shades chosen have a rich base note to add warmth.

■ To add more definition but keep the tonality, one could use a darker, tonal shade of gray as opposed to black.

Mood board see page 187

It was probably the caravans of the Silk Route that brought the idea of marbling to Venice. In the seventeenth century it became so popular it was elevated to the art form that is still synonymous with the city today. Rare texts and books of importance were decorated with exotic marbled endpapers and bound in book cloths that were both distinctive and unique in their design.

This palette draws its inspiration from ancient, precious colors of indigo and lapis, turquoise and aquamarine, jet and citrine, melded together in rhythmic, hypnotic and organic marbled patterns. A rich blue that might otherwise be thoughtlessly denounced as cold, here adroitly refutes the accusation with its very obvious warmth and strength. In fact this palette is almost a lesson in how warm and calming blues can be. As the colors literally dissolve into each other in the marbling tray each one takes on an element of the other, adding to the harmony and enabling you to play with tones and add intensity as needed.

The richness of this palette is deepened by the absence of white in any major form. Instead, a natural linen acts as the neutral base and keeps the palette tonal rather than sharp. Contrast comes in the form of a vivid citrine yellow and turquoise but their sharpness is much mellowed. The overall spirit is intelligent and bookish, serious rather than light-hearted, handsome, calm and more than a little masculine.

Venetian marbling

- A mix of colors such as this works best when you stick to tonality. Keep the palette strict and let the texture do the talking. Matt velvet and shimmering silks will provide contrast and life without altering the balance.

- Using marble as a flat surface is a nod to the roots of the design, giving the surface resonance and a note of humor.

- These tones work best with warm shades of neutral such as gray and taupe, adding space and a sense of light where pure white would be just too bright.

- Accents are easy here: darker tones of cobalt or turquoise, darkest gray for punch and a sharp accent of citrine yellow would add definition and power.

61

flowing pattern with rich textures

Here, the palette is carried through a series of rooms and the colors are used across a variety of textures, from wallpaper to velvet rugs and upholstery to the soft sheen of silk. The overall atmosphere is handsome and rather rich but, given the mix of textures and pattern, beautifully harmonious.

The Arts and Crafts movement, which began in Britain in the late nineteenth century, was an ardent and passionate cry for a return to esthetical beauty, for art and traditional methods of manufacture. It was a direct backlash against the extremes of the Industrial Revolution and favored creativity and craft over speed and machination. The chief protagonists were hugely inspired by nature and the English countryside, the flora and fauna of the British Isles representing a veritable treasure trove of inspiration for their creativity. They repeatedly used flowers and insects as the inspiration and basis for their work.

This palette is inspired by this important movement, which, in turn, inspired the botanical study of butterflies that decorates this room. On a chalky white velvet ground are intricately detailed drawings of moths and butterflies in jade and violet, pearlescent gray and teal blue. These soft and gentle colors provide a relaxing and comforting backdrop in which to live. The delicacy of the neutral shades feels as gracefully fragile as the wings of a butterfly itself. Strength comes in the form of a dark peacock, teal blue that adds definition and refinement without a hint of severity. As such the mix feels airy and light, as soft as a whisper; the chalky white and silvery, pearl gray have an ephemeral lightness, which works off the equally elegant tones of jade. The underlying tones of all the colors are icily cool rather than creamily

arts and crafts

warm and it is this that keeps the scheme floaty and effortless. By using a darker blue as a contrast and defining tool as opposed to black or charcoal, the scheme keeps its lightness in check without the need for hard edges.

- This palette works well in any kind of space: in sunlit, light-filled rooms one can make good use of the chalky white ground. For a richer, cosier feel, add more flannel gray and warm teal.

- Let texture add another layer to the language: further add to the frothy lightness with voiles and silks, or ground the palette with worsted wools and tweeds.

- The use of natural wood in this room adds another nod to the arts and crafts feeling whereas shiny metal or zinc would add a more contemporary, urban feeling.

A chalky ivory white is the main player here, with elegant jade and turquoise adding gentle ethereal touches of lively spirit to the room.

The sights, sounds and scents where land meets sea bring all the senses alive, never failing to inspire: the play of light and shadow on water and shore; the ever-changing colors and movement of the waves; the vast expanse of sea and sky; salty ozone in the air; the hypnotic ebb and flow of the tide. All combine to create a sense of wellbeing and tranquillity that through color and texture can be brought into the home.

Whether the sparkling calm of the Aegean, the translucent shallows of tropical isles or the swirling dark waves of the Atlantic, seascapes can inspire a range of palettes, combinations that are rooted in the most basic of nature's rhythms—the waves of the ocean, travelling for miles and eventually finding land.

In this particular incarnation, the shade of the sea is a glittering tone, somewhere between turquoise and jade, that can be moved and shifted to be more blue or more green depending on your preference. Its partner, the perfect shade of wet sand, acts as a gritty neutral that somehow seems to capture all the elements of gray and taupe so that once again one can shift the balance in either direction at will. It is perhaps fitting that a palette inspired by the movement of water is so intrinsically mobile.

Of course, there is always white, and here it is the white of wave tips and foam as they meet the shore. There are no sharp accents or bright jolts of contrast; instead a timeless, spellbinding mix of simple shades.

seashore

- Because the blue is the only point of color in the palette it is critical to get it right. For a more jade tone, balance it with gray. If leaning more to blue, use a truer shade of sandstone or taupe to create that ubiquitous seashore feeling.

- Keep your white in tune with both colors and remember it should work easily with your chosen blue/green or gray/taupe. It is the white that adds definition in this scheme, keeping it light and effortless.

- If you want to add punch use a stronger shade of the blue/green rather than adding a contrasting accent.

- Natural textures such as sandstone or plaster, limestone and marble are easy partners for hard surfaces within this palette. Shimmering silk and velvet also perfectly capture the ocean's luminosity.

The shades of the seashore are among the most relaxing to live with.
Keep the palette tonal but play with texture for added depth.

celadon and jade

In my view there are few more relaxing colors to live with than the glassy, delicate, aqua tones that blur the fringes of blue and green. This palette is inspired by the soft shades of ancient Chinese celadon glazed ceramics and precious jade. Translucent yet less transparent and more substantial than those of the Seashore palette on page 68, these colors are easy-going but also possess an innate elegance that perfectly balances formality with insouciance. They are also incredibly versatile: naturally at home in a contemporary setting or equally suited to a traditional scheme.

Although apparently cool, in reality these colors are anything but—used with soft neutrals like parchment and linen they feel more gentle and warm than their perceived glassy coolness. Put them with clear white and even tones of gray and the mood can change again to a modern feel. In this room, vivacious accents of soft apple green punctuate the ethereal stillness of the jade and celadon. A soft warm white further accentuates the light airiness that is this palette's signature.

- This palette is all about lightness and airiness, so avoid choosing heavy dark tones for definition. Instead use white or a slightly deeper tone of the jade to highlight and add detail.

- Texture is the perfect way to add warmth and richness with these colors: a velvet and linen damask does this at a stroke without compromising the delicacy of the palette.

- Manipulating the colors via different textures further calls to mind celadon glaze and the luminous quality of jade.

- Shiny reflective hard surfaces— marble, plastic, metal and glass— work beautifully with this palette, allowing light to bounce around the space in different ways.

relaxed formality

In this light and airy sitting room the palette
is used to great effect. High ceilings and a
white on white floral paper add to the feeling
of elegant lightness, whilst soft textures of
washed velvet, linen and sturdy cotton add
warmth and richness. Pattern is kept simple
with classic damasks at the windows
and on the sofa.

In Chinese culture, choosing color is not always a straightforward process. The very nature of color represents not only centuries of mystery and meaning, of custom and tradition, but the colors themselves are layered with symbolism. In the theory of the five elements, different colors represent an emotional state as well as their own natural element. Green symbolizes health, prosperity and harmony, spring and wood. Red represents good fortune, luck, happiness and fire. However it is yellow that is considered the zenith of the color wheel in Chinese culture—the prestigious color of Imperial China; palaces and emperors, the yin and the yang, of stability; in fact the very center of being. It represents the earth.

This palette takes its cue from the art of Chinese landscape painting and is inspired by the reflections of willow leaves in watery pools. The sharp acidity of the Chinese yellow is balanced by gentler tones of olive and grass green while pure alabaster white further diffuses but does not inhibit its power. A watery tone of lead gray works brilliantly as a neutral, adding gravity to what could be seen to be a frivolous group.

Definition comes in the form of graphic charcoal—the darkest possible tone of gray, just before black and echoing the inky darkness of the artist's brush. An outright black would be too harsh and alter the harmonious balance. The presence of jade green evokes an ethereal feeling of nostalgia, working with the yellow to create a dynamic and lively feeling. The whole

reflections of China

palette comes into focus with the addition of a vivid rose pink. At a stroke, it adds warmth and contrast and is suitably romantic and light whereas a rich red or orange, say, would overpower. The palette now is perfectly balanced: yin and yang in perfect harmony.

- For a sharper more contemporary look, stick to the key colors of yellow, jade, pink and graphite with white and omit the diffusing tones of olive, gray and grass green.

- The palette is by nature sharp, so if you want to use it in a space where light is cold or indeed limited, then make sure you use a warmer tone of white and use more grass green rather than the naturally cool jade.

- Make the palette even more romantic by increasing the intensity and presence of the pink and using yellow more as an accent.

Plain interesting textures give balance and harmony to a space allowing a beautiful pattern to breathe...

mixing texture, pattern and plains
This palette is elegant and timeless, yet also lends itself to use in a contemporary setting. In this tall-ceilinged airy room, plain fabrics in all the background shades of green and gray draw attention to the drop of pattern at the windows, where the full palette is used. Ubiquitous tones of jade and Chinese yellow come together with charcoal, dove gray, olive green, chalk white and a vibrant rose pink, giving the space a mysteriously Oriental flavor.

From the early seventeenth century, a succession of intrepid and daring botanists traveled to far-flung corners of the globe in search of undiscovered and exotic species of flora and fauna. These valiant explorers often traveled at great personal risk and were utterly fearless in their quest to find new species and be the first to record them for posterity. Their finds formed the mainstay of private and public collections such as those held by London's Royal Botanical Gardens at Kew or Le Jardin du Roi in Paris (now known as the Jardin des Plantes). Once collected, specimens were carefully recorded in meticulous and highly detailed illustrative drawings from which the species could be identified, observed and studied. In every sense, these pioneering innovators were at the vanguard of discovery and the trend hunters of their day.

This palette takes its cue from this extraordinary period in time and is inspired by the plants and flowers of the era. A monochrome black and white forms the structure of the scheme, reminiscent of the intricate ink and pencil drawings of the botanists. Timeless yet entirely contemporary at the same time, the black and white is the perfect backdrop on which to layer more color. A lush and vivid leafy green is the next important shade and although almost as neutral as its monochrome partners adds vitality and personality. This nearly neutral trio is countered by further joyful tones of rich zinnia, peony pink, the mauve of royal tulips and a vibrant citrus yellow. Every one of these shades on its own is strong and full of character, yet their natural exuberance is kept in check by the studious pairing of black and white

modern botanical

and tempered by the lively green. The palette's success depends on the careful balance of all these elements. Here, it is incorporated within the drapes and echoed on various accessories while every other element is either monochrome or green, evoking a spirit of vitality that in no way clashes or jars.

■ Firstly, identify the right white and black pairing. Creamy toned whites have a more traditional quality, whereas a sharper blue-based white will feel cooler and more modern. Just as there are many shades of white, there are also many shades of black. Get this right and it will underpin everything else.

■ Besides using black and white as the base of the scheme, employ touches of it throughout your room. Consider it for rugs, cushions or picture frames. This pairing provides the continuity that allows the other colors to sing without dominating or clashing.

■ Consider which accent colors you wish to use and keep all of them within the same tonal family so they do not fight one another.

Murano glass

For centuries, the artisan glass blowers of the island of Murano in the Venetian lagoon have perfected their art and captivated the world with their hand-blown, intensely colored and luminous glassware. The Venetians color their glass with confidence and dexterity, often mixing striking elements such as aquamarine, cobalt and ultramarine with emerald, viridian and crimson in one piece to great effect.

It is this radiant form of art that has inspired this palette. Here a wondrous mix of turquoise and ultramarine combine with a soft sky blue, leaf green and acid green for a rich and modern combination of colors. The turquoise is a singing vibrant tone and deeper than the others in the palette which lends it a dominance and power that defines the scheme. The other elements of softer sky and leaf provide an easy backdrop from which the star of the show shines. With this palette, texture can play an even greater part in bringing the mix to life—an iridescent and complex velvet in turquoise and

ultramarine shimmers against the flatter tones of sky and leaf linen. A dazzling white adds sharpness and light and stands up to the force of the turquoise. Another velvet in iridescent acid green both links to the blues but also adds a counterpoint and contrast.

As a backdrop to the palette in this room, the walls are covered with a speckled marbled paper that elegantly mixes shades of white, aqua, steel gray and touches of silver—thus setting the tone of the palette in one stroke. A platinum gray rug adds definition and grounds the scheme adding just enough definition and focus.

- Instead of the shimmering richness of velvet, a silk or satin would work equally well with this palette.

- With this palette for greater depth use a darker tone of gray blue, which will also toughen up the scheme and add punch.

Vivid, verdant shades of jade and dark sea-green are lightened with silvery gray—as ethereal as white with an additional pearly delicacy.

mid-century modern

The 1950s was a defining moment in so many aspects of design. Fashion and architecture, industrial and product design are just some of the disciplines that benefitted from the new mood and energy that imbued the post-war world. Modernity was defined during this time by designers like Charles and Ray Eames, Aalto, Saarinen, Jacobsen and Knoll, whose groundbreaking ideas produced work of startling originality. In interiors, colors ranged from shiny pops of primary red and white to a more moody, masculine and natural style.

It is the latter that has inspired this particular palette—a rich earthy olive green, charcoal gray and emerald are the key players, offering a mood of perfectly balanced restraint and dynamism. Serious charcoal and restrained olive are lifted by dynamic pops of emerald and fennel while darkest graphite gives definition and sharpness. Shades of gray provide the neutral backbone, evoking black-and-white photography and further underlining the palette's almost bookish tone.

In this room, a spark of modernity is visible in the gleaming light fitting and polished concrete floor. Textures are soft and tactile—plush, matt velvets and tweed—while pattern is kept simple, geometric and almost abstract so that no one element dominates and there is space to reflect and contemplate.

- This palette relies on all the colors working together from the same tonal group—no sharp jolts of contrast here. Rather, think definition and deepen your neutral to its darkest.

- Keep details simple and unadorned to maintain the mid-century mood: white walls and wooden furniture add further 50's details. Wool tweeds and simple textures also work well here.

mid-century modern greens

In this cool, modern open-plan living area light bounces off the hard surfaces of polished concrete, glass and dark wood furniture, whilst a rich mix of greens and grays in woven texture and pattern bring notes of interest to the monochrome setting.

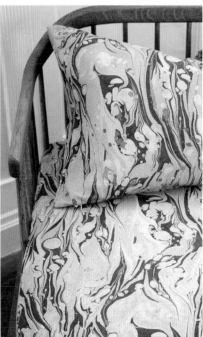

Mood board see page 187

Umbria in spring

The countryside of Umbria holds a special place in my heart: mile after mile of rolling hills and fields; ancient hilltop villages and towns interspersed with olive groves and orchards. It is a land still dedicated to nature: to sowing, growing and harvesting in tune with the cycle of the seasons—and spring is its invitation to the dance. After what may seem like an interminable winter of silvery frosts, leaden skies and dormant land, the sun returns and, almost overnight, the landscape comes magically to life. As the seasons shift, nature delivers a new color palette: vitality comes dressed in shades of lush green, the color of life. A sharp and vibrant almost acid green is the first color of tender new growth, followed by a singing emerald and shining shades of bright apple and grass.

It is often said that there are no color clashes in nature and, although there are times when I might disagree, in this vista there is nothing but harmony. Lit by the golden glow of the sun, the many shades of green flow into each other with ease, punctuated by the evergreen of Cypress trees, stone villages and terracotta tiled towns.

If you are as intoxicated as I am by the joy of spring, this palette is truly wonderful to live with. The shades of green are strong and quite vivid, but their harmonious tones make them almost impossible to get wrong. The neutral base is, as always, important; in this instance it appears as an earthy natural stone rather than a brighter white or gray.

It is crucial to get this right as its warmth underpins the whole mood. Temper the mix with a rich, dark brown or darkest charcoal, reminiscent of the bark of trees, and use an old white to add space and a breath of freshness. No sharp contrasts are needed here as the shades of green fill your space with warmth and energy, celebrating the beauty and mystery of nature.

- As always, identify your neutral base colors first as these are critical to the success of the scheme. If all your greens are yellow-based and your neutral is blue-based, you will not find the harmony that is this palette's signature.

- Stick to the same tonal family but go green with confidence and use layers of color for interest.

- If you are keen to mix patterns, then stick to a simple palette of colors or the room will feel overwhelming.

Brecon hills

The Brecon Beacons in South Wales is a glorious area of soaring mountains and glittering lakes; rocky outcrops, woods and hills in every verdant shade of green. On this misty canvas, nature paints farmland and hills in cool tones of slate gray, natural linen, moss green and misty blue while the myriad colors in rock and stone gleam in the watery light. The scene is coolly restful, restorative and also ruggedly masculine. It is this almost mythical landscape that inspires this palette.

The mix is predominantly taken from the cool end of the spectrum: as demonstrated in this room a fresh shade of natural stone is the backdrop—a whitened, almost gray shade that has a lightness and ease but is cool in its undertone. Rather than making this south-facing room feel cold it subtly balances the light, giving the space an atmosphere of reflective simplicity. Tweed fabrics are a natural choice here and heathery mixes of graphite and stone, dove gray and chalk, grass green and pebble provide lively yet plain expanses of color.

Texture also comes in the form of natural linen, its scoured sturdiness further adding to the utilitarian ruggedness of the scheme. Dark wood and bark brown lend definition, providing strength and substance while remaining in keeping with the naturalness of the palette. The feeling is contemplative yet strong.

- This palette is all about creating and working with cooler natural shades, so to keep the look strong and tonal don't be tempted to add warm contrasts.

- Keep your mix slightly on the gray side and let the textures you choose warm up or further cool down the mix. Here, soft velvet echoes the moss of the mountains, providing warmth and softness.

- Use natural elements like wood, slate, glass or stone that underline the natural rugged beauty of the scheme.

Nothing evokes a refreshing zing like a slice of bright citrus; its sharp acidity adds vitality and vivacity as easily as a spritz of lemon or lime to a sparkling drink. It can lift the spirits, bring in warm sunshine and is a wonderful way of perking up a scheme composed mainly of neutrals.

The starting point for this palette was a vivid alchemilla-painted wall set against the lush backdrop of a verdant walled garden in India, the jolt of citrus adding a sharp modernity and providing a pop of focus among the many shades of green. A shade such as this is no shy wallflower; it is used primarily for its attention-seeking properties. However, when used in conjunction with the other colors in the palette, these properties recede while at the same time the sharp color continues to deliver its particular brand of vitality and punch.

Without this alchemilla accent the palette is strict and on the masculine side; shades of gray—concrete, graphite and dove— are tempered with masses of white and a forest green, but it is the zingy citrus that makes the whole combination come alive.

Texture is at the forefront here, softening what might otherwise be seen as a rather masculine space. The sofa is upholstered in a sturdy tweed in which accents of vibrant citrus add punch to its many neutral shades. A stool is upholstered in a soft geometric velvet; a shiny version of the shade is used on a small table, while tiny vibrant notes of citrus draw attention to cushions, vases, plants and throws scattered throughout the room. The resulting lightness of touch and modernity bring to life what would otherwise be rather a subdued scheme. Muted green, soft chalky grays and white provide the neutral balance.

neutrals with zing

This particular room has plenty of light, but in a darker room the same palette could be employed just as effectively.

- Instead of white walls, use one of the shades of gray or even the darker bottle green for drama. Remember, a small, dark room painted white remains exactly that —white can help but it will not magically create the illusion of light or space where there is none.

- In warmer climates, where there is plenty of light, use the palest gray on the walls to add a crisp finish and keep the palette light, but intensify the tone of citrus to stand up to the light.

- Use more of the darker gray and you will add gravity to the interior; it will feel richer and more dramatic while retaining its somewhat masculine edge.

citrine and emerald balance gray and stone

In this contemporary, yet comfortable open plan living area, the palette is used to great effect—the colors orchestrated via surface and texture rather than paint or paper. The elements of nature play a huge part: natural bleached wood, glass, stone and brick give the space a distinctly organic, almost puritanical air, the palette reflecting this but also echoing the cool greens from the garden beyond.

97

In the summer of 1925 the French government sponsored a rather special exhibition. Held in over fifty-five acres in the centre of Paris, the Exposition Internationale des Arts Décoratifs et Industriels Modernes heralded a new design movement. The rules of the exhibition clearly stated that all work had to be modern; no historical styles were permitted. The purpose was to unite modernity with craftsmanship and to highlight French leadership in the manufacture of luxury furniture, porcelain, glass, metalwork, textiles and other decorative products. To further promote the movement, all the major Paris department stores opened design and decorative arts sections and four new French ocean liners were decorated in the new style.

This style became known as Art Deco and it was revolutionary, replacing the curving organic lines of Art Nouveau which preceded it; Art Deco was the epitome of modernity: streamlined and straight lined, elegant and glamorous, it was a breath of fresh air and affected every aspect of modern life until World War II.

It is this innate glamour and elegance that was the inspiration for this palette. Cool steely gray and white form the backbone; the white signifying modernity and the gray a nod to the industrialism and mechanization that so influenced the esthetic. A sophisticated, optimistic shade of yellow adds a note of exuberance, while a darker gray and charcoal add graphic touches. The palette is kept purposefully tight and plays perfectly to its 20's roots—modern and restrained yet self-assured and nonchalant too.

In this Parisian apartment, the palette is limited to bold blocks of color with just the glamour of the silk drapes adding pattern.

Parisian chic

- Texture can play a vital part in making this palette work in a variety of spaces. Velvet and silk, wool and satin are all deco textures that will add interest and vitality to your space.

- Don't be tempted to add too many notes of contrast to this scheme—you will undermine its simplicity, which is its calling card. If you must add in tonal shades take the yellow into leaf green and the charcoal gray into steel. Remember, less is more.

- Use the white that works best in your room and then choose your tone of gray and yellow. A sharp lemon might work brilliantly in a sunny south-facing room but could appear harsh where there is less light.

- The palette is neither overtly masculine nor feminine but could be taken further in either direction: increase and strengthen the gray for a more masculine take.

woodland spring

I consider myself very fortunate to live in a country that has distinct seasons, the ever-changing landscape always alive with new possibilities. I love them all for different reasons but spring is probably my favorite. In temperate climes, after the trials of a long winter, I adore the feeling of a fresh start and renewal, not to mention the clarity of early spring colors that revitalize the landscape with new growth—snowdrops, daffodils, leaves and buds that hint at what is yet to come from nature. In shady woods, tiny yellow celandine and aconite flowers emerge from the earth with myriad green leaves to herald the end of winter.

This palette is inspired by that magical time of year: softest shades of pale birch and stone, wild hellebore and primrose are delicate yet positive reminders of those first shafts of spring sunlight. The feeling of calm relaxation they evoke also makes them peaceful yet refreshing colors to live with. As always, getting the neutrals right is important. Soft shades of bark and pebble lend warmth and softness while a chalk white has just the right amount of sharpness to add contrast. The freshest of greens adds a lively dynamism, accentuated by a sharper note of lemony yellow. The scheme is an exercise in balance and restraint—temper the sharpness with soft neutrals and let the optimistic shades of primrose and cardamom pod add the vitality.

- This palette works beautifully in any room. Use texture to add warmth as needed. In this room, softly diaphanous curtains further filter the light and add to the delicate mood.

- If you would like to make this palette more masculine, and even a little urban, increase the use and shades of pebble and birch. Use plain, classic textures such as velvet or linen to accentuate the palette.

There is a wonderful dreamy quality to this palette: use it to infuse any room with a sense of calm.

summer sorbet

This delicate palette is inspired by the subtle shades of iced fruit sorbets on a hot summer's day. Cool tones of mint and rose, vanilla and pistachio are as light as a breeze and capture an elegance and subtlety that feels understated and unusual.

The defining base color is a romantic one—soft, creamy, vanilla yellow. Used on its own, this shade could feel rather nostalgic and perhaps a little old fashioned, but in this palette the lightest touches of watery jade and celadon add a delicate freshness and coolness that immediately sharpens the mood and updates it. Further romance is added with soft shades of rose pink and watermelon, but these shades are also sharp and clear so cut through the rich vanilla with a lightness of touch, while adding a subtle prettiness that feels modern.

Graceful and refined, the palette feels lively rather than over sweet, its freshness due to the cool undertones of jade and mint, rose and pistachio.

A crisp clear white is used as the neutral of choice and, as always, adds light and space in an instant.

- This palette works brilliantly in light-filled, sunny rooms but can just as easily be used in a room with a colder light. Balance a warmer tone of vanilla and rose, but retain the cooler elements of jade and mint for the same refreshing feeling.

- To give the palette more depth you could add deeper shades of birch or cocoa which will fit well in the mix as well as adding strength.

Mood board see page 188

In this light and airy drawing room the romantic combination of colors feels relaxed, easy and contemporary.

celebrating flowers

For thousands of years, flowers have been used as symbols of thanksgiving and celebration and as a way of expressing the purest form of human emotion. To those who love them, they represent an almost primal shorthand that goes to the very heart of an emotion without the need for words, actions or even presence. The way flowers are put together can be as arresting as the most powerful art and as lyrical as the most beautiful poetry; and when brought into an interior—either living or represented in wallpaper and furnishings—they can create or change the mood of a room in an instant.

Spirited and joyful, this palette is a celebration of the beauty of flowers at their extravagant best. Vibrant and vivid colors come together to express the extraordinary vitality of nature. Shocking pink, bright yellow, sky blue and a delicate leaf green are balanced with more subtle shades of soft pink, teal and copper. A cool gray and the softest white provide a clear neutral base, allowing the colors to sing, while a darker gray and a moss green add a more moody note that reins in the exuberance of the brighter shades.

This palette is a master class in balance and proportion: the more subtle counterparts allow the brights their moment in the spotlight, while ensuring they are seen not as naive stabs but as celebratory notes in a symphony of color.

Take care not to tip the balance in either direction or you will lose that unbridled spirit of joy and celebration.

- In this room the palette is mainly visible in the wallpaper and drapes, with different shades picked out as highlights; this keeps the rhythm of the floral palette lively. To shift the emphasis you could use shades of gray or soft white on upholstery and employ the accent colors on throws or cushions.

- The brighter accent colors in this palette could dominate and overwhelm every other ingredient, but if carefully matched with a steady hand of deeper richer tones, they become highlights rather than the stars.

- The neutrals in this palette are very soft, the gentle tones of the ivory white and pale gray diffusing the colors, lending a more serious note to balance the brights.

Use this palette of spirited, joyful, confident colors to create rooms with a strong sense of vitality and energy.

110

111

vintage roses

The rose is without doubt seen by many as the enduring symbol of romance and love and has justly inspired many of our collections. More often than not, I am on the side of modernity, looking forwards rather than back; for some reason I always feel a sense of nostalgia in a rose garden, so they are not among my favorite flowers. But I am also fascinated by how colors can instantly evoke a mood or a moment in time, just by their tonality, and the soft colors and shapes of old roses can do just that in a room.

In this palette I wanted to create a feeling of romance, but without overt sentimentality or fustiness, just a comforting beauty that feels relaxed, easy and timeless. Soft tints of rose and petal pink are balanced with earthy and gentle sage green, mint and olive. No sharp white for contrast or crisp sharpness here, instead dreamy, creamy neutrals provide the background to the palette. The feeling is informal, further underlined by the use of casual linen textures too.

- A soft, mellow white could also feel harmonious here, providing just enough freshness to enhance the romance of the mood.

- Off-beat colors such as a warm soft denim blue would also work well here —this would toughen up the palette without dominating.

- Textures, like color, alter the mood of a space, so for a more formal feel consider a cotton satin or silk or velvet instead of the more casual tumbled linen.

- Just as in a rose garden, the use of green adds vitality and depth. For a more spirited and modern feel one could use a sharper, more lime green.

113

Soft moss green and rose pink, with buttery neutrals, feel relaxed and cosily classic in this sunny sitting room.

115

The softest hints of color create an atmosphere of meditative calm in this elegant space.

vellum and parchment

Decorating with neutral shades can often seem like an easy option. It may feel safer to sidestep the seemingly tricky balancing act of using stronger colors, which can appear to be fraught with difficulties and possible errors of judgement. Yet, the truth is, it can be much more difficult to decorate with neutral colors. There can be many pitfalls—neutrals clash just as much as any other colors and, in so doing, can appear flat, dull and unattractive. The very mistakes one is trying to avoid by playing safe with color can ironically come to pass.

However, neutral shades can be a joy to live with; I have always loved their gentle and contemplative nature. But in my view, in order for the scheme to work, it is vital that a positive mood is created, which comes from positive color choices rather than a default, playing-it-safe approach.

This palette is unashamedly neutral and dreamily so. Shades of parchment and vellum, soft birch and doeskin are used with off white and the palest, barely there shell pink, vanilla, a soft green and pebble gray. The mood thereby created is relaxing and meditative, but there is an underlying vitality that makes its presence felt without dominating in any way.

- In south-facing, light-filled rooms, you can use much more off white and parchment for lightness. This can easily be tempered in rooms with less light where you can add richness by letting the doeskin and birch take charge.

- The soft pink underlines the gentle nature of the scheme and adds a note of surprising prettiness.

- The underlying tones of these colors are warm, enhancing the mood of reflection without compromising the uplifting feel of the contemporary scheme.

117

Irish linen

Ireland is known throughout the world as the Emerald Isle, and for good reason. From the air, its fields and glens, valleys and mountains do indeed seem to be clothed in the brightest of verdant velvet. However on closer inspection, it is a land of many more colors and subtle tones. Its landscapes are far-reaching and varied, none more so than in County Kerry. There, majestic mountains of darkest purple-brown granite meet the steely blue-gray Atlantic Ocean on beaches that are scattered with rocks and pebbles in tones of faded heather, sand and slate blue-gray. It is this surprising combination of natural colors that inspires this earthy palette.

The underlying tones here are rich and warm and it is this depth that adds complexity rather than austerity—no bursts of pure strong color, rather a series of gentle hues and half tones that melt from one to another and dissolve harmoniously therein. Texture is vital to this palette as it is these soft natural materials that provide the dynamic in the space. Heavy linens in misty tones juxtapose with finer weights in stone, pebble and quartz.

- A sharp white works well here, adding a slice of modernity and crispness. If you prefer to keep the palette suitably cloudy then use a gentler off-white neutral instead.

Italian marble

Surprising as it may seem with my reputation for working with vibrant strong colors, I am a great fan of neutral rooms. They can be easy and chic and appear effortlessly stylish—but equally, they can look lifeless, flat and rather dull. In my view the trick is to make your neutral scheme alive and interesting, with a definite personality, rather than merely safe.

For centuries, Italy has been famous for its quarries: Carrara, Botticino, Pavonazzo and Siena marbles all harness the beauty of their natural landscapes and add a stroke of classical, neutral luxury when used in interiors.

This palette is an ode to stylish neutrality: where the Vellum and Parchment palette on page 117 is soft and meditative, here the mood is sophisticated and smart, awash with reflected light from hard surfaces and the sheen of patterned fabrics. Shades veer from cool stone and plaster through to travertine, marble and alabaster, all with a tonal quality that links them together and keeps the overall mood

calm and collected. The effect is enlivened by metallic and contrasting textures, adding a dynamic note and keeping the mix lively. Softly shimmering velvets and damasks catch the light in different ways, as do metallic touches on the walls, while marble, plaster and natural cane underline the palette and ensure the mood is easy.

- To maintain the balance, use deeper tones of your neutrals to add definition and detail.

- Take care when choosing the colors of your surfaces, furniture and electrical goods—a large expanse of black would be far too harsh here and upset the careful balance. Instead look at white or possibly brushed aluminum.

- Touches of green bring life to any palette. A stroke of leaf or grass green works particularly well with other neutrals.

natural alabaster and travertine

In this elegant morning room, shades of those natural marbles and travertine bring a delicate sophistication to the space. The palette is cool and restrained but here, texture and pattern conduct a spirited dialogue between the relative shades, adding vivacity. The underlying chalky white links all the other neutral shades, so the overall effect is quietly joyful.

modern mono-chrome

The black-and-white palette is as timeless and classic as civilization itself: think black coal and white embers, black ink on white paper, chalk on a blackboard, the printed word, black-and-white films and artists' sketches; the list goes on. It is almost as though monochrome and the tones that separate its two opposite parts is not really a palette at all, but rather a default option that we turn to when we are unsure of treading a more "interesting" path. But that would be to greatly underestimate what this combination can do.

Black and white together will always add a degree of graphic detail, a sharp defining edge and is classically chic yet simultaneously undeniably contemporary. It is vital when using black and white together to get both colors right and ensure that your base tone throughout is harmonious. For example, it would be foolish to assume that all whites are the same: of course they are not, there are many different shades and they can clash. Think of the cold blue-white of ice and snow, the yellow-white of milk and cream, the greenish tints of white in wild garlic flowers or spring apple blossom. They are all white, yet they can clash in a much more strident and jarring way than some other colors.

Just as there are shades of white, there are also shades of black: consider the blue-black of a raven's wing compared with the warmer shade of graphite or lamp black, the earthiness of ebony compared with the luminous quality of jet. So the trick here is to unite your underlying base tones. The best way to do this is to use samples of fabric and wallpaper, cover large pieces of card with paint, then put them all together. Instantly you will see which shades feel harmonious and which just look and feel "wrong".

- Black and white is ubiquitous and can literally be used anywhere, but choosing the right shades of black and white is crucial. A sharp, clear white and black feels powerful, timeless and strong, whereas a softer white and charcoal is a gentler incarnation of monochrome.

- Texture is perhaps more important than ever when using monochrome—a play of different surfaces will add that all-important personality and vivacity to a scheme. Mix tweeds with silk, wools and linens, velvet and print, while keeping the palette tight.

- This palette is a wonderful choice for displaying artwork or groups of collections like ceramics or glassware. Its monochromatic graphicness perfectly bookends your displays, allowing them to shine.

125

Plain most certainly need not mean dull: a mix of interesting, tactile textures playing off each other gives this space a smart, dynamic energy.

surface and texture

This open-plan Danish apartment is an exercise in monochromatic restraint. Classic tongue-and-groove panelling is painted a soft white while the floor is a dark graphite. Light bounces off the white surface and details are picked out in the same palette with a tasteful mix of textures. The atmosphere is smart and contemplative which is further enhanced by the absence of any overt pattern—just simple sturdy textures offering warmth and comfort with a touch of monochrome strictness.

black +
white =
gray

A monochrome palette of black and white is ideally suited to a working space or when you are after that smart, contemporary sharpness, yet perhaps less appropriate for an inviting living space. But when one starts to blur the edges, life gets interesting: various tones and shades of gray will soften the sharpness of black and white, add dignity and gravity, or introduce moods that can lift the spirits and feel as joyous as if you were using a colorful palette.

This palette harnesses all the power and graphic detail of black and white but adds softer edges and warmth with tones of cloudy gray, charcoal and mist. The trick here is to pinpoint the deepest shade of charcoal/black you would like to use and then, staying in the same tone, go to the other end of the spectrum and identify the softest shade of white. Now fill in with some mid tones of gray and employ pattern and texture in your chosen shades to give your room vitality and energy.

The simplicity of monochrome and its clear natural boundaries allows you to layer scales of patterns and texture without overwhelming a space, provided you stick to the palette.

- This palette feels restful and easy: to keep it that way, don't be tempted to add accent colors or notes of contrast.

- Black, white and gray can work anywhere: in sunny light-filled rooms use light, soft textiles such as translucent linen and cotton voiles. In cooler rooms, where you may want a cosier feeling, velvet and wool flannel will add warmth.

- By nature this palette can seem serious: to lighten the mood, increase the use of plain white which will highlight details and add a softer feeling.

- For a more masculine, urban feel, add more dark gray or black.

a monochrome mix of patterns and plains

In this beautiful, eclectic sitting room the palette is employed in every possible way, from floor to walls to furnishings. The mix of patterns and textures adds vivacity and a sense of fun without feeling frivolous or indeed particularly feminine. In this instance, it is the use of plains that defines details. A reversible plain cushion breaks up the pattern and provides breathing space. Likewise a plain shaded curtain and a self-patterned rug do the same.

130

London skyline

I suppose if you were to give London a color it would have to be gray. A trip down the River Thames on a wintry day reveals gray in myriad different shades: it colors the pavements and buildings, bridges and public spaces, the river itself and, more often than not, the London sky. It is an urban color and to live it is to love it! And to consider it dull would be to vastly underestimate it: gray is every bit as multi-faceted as the city that inspires this palette.

For me, London is one of the world's most exciting cities. A vibrant centre for culture, creativity and the arts, it also has a breathless appetite for consumerism and consumption. Its energy and dynamic pace of life is fast and furious but sometimes unforgiving and, as such, living in the city requires a home that is a haven, a place where one can wind down and relax.

This cool loft brings in the colors from outside, tempering the monochrome palette with a softness that makes it easy to live with.

Shades of graphite and charcoal, platinum and silver, flannel and concrete work well together, and the vitality of the room comes from all the different textures and patterns.

- The trick here is to unite all the shades by their underlying tonality: in this instance, shades that have a clear blue/gray tone which feels contemporary and crisp.

- By keeping the structure white, using color and pattern solely on fabrics and rugs, the space feels light and spacious but intimate at the same time.

- The palette is united and tight, so textures and patterns can be mixed with abandon, in the safe knowledge that they will add interest whilst remaining harmonious. Rather like London itself.

- Use more dark graphite to add definition and white to add light and a sense of space.

133

winter
smoke

Black, white, gray and neutral shades working together can be rich and warm, cool and calm. They can feel expansive and open or cosy and cosseting; dynamic and vital or pure and simple —the trick is to put them together in a way that makes them interesting. It is also important to pay attention to the exact shades you use, making sure the underlying tones of each shade work together.

In this scheme the feeling is one of rich formality and luxurious warmth. Dark, smoky grays are juxtaposed with lighter tones of the same colors. Almost like a wash of watercolor or Japanese ink, the tones are derived from each other to ensure they will work in harmony. The feeling is moody and mysterious, masculine and strong. There are no obvious counterpoints of contrast but rather highlights come in the form of a silvery white and platinum that add a shimmer and lightness to the space.

Texture here is crucial. In this dark, north-facing sitting room we have chosen to work with the moodiness, but to create a feeling of luxury and softness we have used luxurious and soft textures that in themselves provide contrast. Rich woven shaded velvets work beautifully with shimmering silk satins that in turn add glossy lustre to the matt texture. Pattern adds another dimension, with graphic checks and geometrics providing a layer of lively interest that ensures the scheme doesn't look stuffy or safe.

- Black or white adds definition to the scheme: use it to underline a detail or in order to add depth.

- This palette can work just as well in a sunny climate or a light-filled room. Swap the richer textures for lighter linens and voiles, use flatter textures like cotton and canvas and keep the highlight with silk.

- In a space with more light, use the palest shade of gray as your anchor and let the darker tones provide a counterpoint and contrast.

Dark and moody meets classic luxury: mix sumptuous velvets and shimmering silks and keep your palette restrained for rich formality.

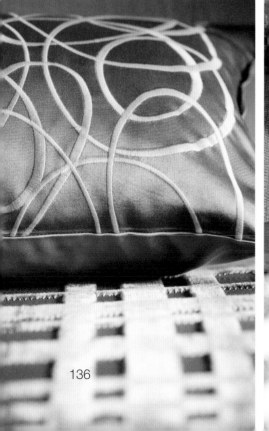

The quiet stillness in the work of the Danish painter Vilhelm Hammershøi has long held a fascination for many; not for nothing was an exhibition of his work entitled *The Poetry of Silence*. Softly lit and with a mastery of tinted shades and tones, his paintings evoke a particular mood of mystery and serenity. Through his eyes, the everyday subjects he painted took on an air of studied simplicity. So finely detailed that some pictures could be mistaken for photographs, they all possess the same sense of distant, meditative calm. His work can be every bit as hypnotic as that of Mark Rothko or Howard Hodgkin with their use of intense colors. In fact it is the very absence of strong color that lends his work its stillness. Immersing oneself in a Hammershøi is akin to pausing for a moment, taking a breath, rebalancing.

For every strong palette or collection, there are equally compelling reasons to create something softer and quieter, the other side of the coin perhaps. Hammershøi deliberately reduced his own palette of colors so that nothing could diminish the influence of Nordic light, to allow for greater artistic improvisation. It is this powerful combination of soft light and pared-back color that has inspired this palette.

Here, barely there tints melt into each other in moody pools of gray and mauve, lilac, chalk, petrol blue and soft sage. At first sight, the palette appears to be cool and clear, yet the atmosphere is anything but. The colors may be from the cooler side of the spectrum but their underlying tones are warm and full of richness. The effect is a perfect balance of controlled stillness and softness.

colors of silence

As is often the case, it is crucial to identify your neutral bases—the lightness of touch in this palette comes from the softest whisper of gray and chalky white, whereas a taupe or stony natural would feel heavy and weigh the palette down. Definition comes in the form of a rich petrol blue, itself a color whose boundaries are softly blurred between blue and green. Its inky softness provides a perfect contrast to the chalk and gray, while the other tints fill in the gaps. The palette has a serenity and softness that is timeless and elegantly chic.

- Remember that whites can clash, so once you have found your perfect soft white stick with it. Any degree of yellow in this palette would alter the balance and "dirty" the lightness.

- Make the palette more feminine by increasing the use of lilac. Similarly, you could toughen up the palette by adding touches of denim that would also add a youthful note.

- Don't be tempted to add any strong notes of contrast: this palette is all about tonal harmony. Instead, for more strength use darker tones of the palette.

Petrol blue meets misty mauve, lilac and chalky white in this ethereal dreamy space. These colors evoke clarity, serenity and calm.

141

The ancient stone villages and hilltop towns of Provence in the South of France have a personality and identity all their own. On the hillsides, the heady smell of pine and wild herbs scent the air, while in the valleys, field upon field of lavender color the landscape a warm mauve. In the height of summer, the landscape resembles a tapestry of blue-mauve mixed with the pale straw of intermittent wheat fields and shades of green from olive, pine and Cypress trees. The old buildings' thick walls of plaster and stone provide a welcome barrier to the baking heat outside. It is a timeless, evocative and languorous landscape that has inspired artists for generations.

This palette recreates that soft, dreamy landscape with its neutral base of plaster and chalk, tints of mauve, lilac and dusky purple. It has a coolness that is the perfect foil to heat, so works brilliantly in sun-drenched rooms or hot climates. However, in rooms that naturally feel cooler it can be used with confidence with some simple tweaks. The main color in the scheme is a pale yet earthy shade of mauve; it's a reflective and gentle shade and one that can be manipulated to appear more masculine or feminine—choose a more gray-based mauve or one that has more pinky beige undertones accordingly.

old Provence

The beauty of the palette depends very much on the harmonious tones that underpin it, definition and accents come in the form of a darker shade of violet and gray and a dark bottle green. Here the warm stony neutral of choice echoes the sandy chalk paths that run between the lavender bushes. Like the rest of the palette, it carefully treads a tightrope between warm and cool and is perfectly balanced. The softness of the ecru keeps the whole feeling dreamy and gentle and any white within this scheme should be a warm one to maintain the balance.

■ To make this palette work in a
   darker north-facing room, use a
   warmer-based mauve.

■ Texture is a brilliant way of adding
   warmth without compromising on the
   tones: rich velvets and shaded wools
   will automatically add depth.

■ For a more urban or masculine feel,
   try increasing the use of dark gray.

Dutch
flowers

During the seventeenth century, the Netherlands experienced a Golden Age of painting. The subject matter was varied but some of the most popular were still lives: sensuous and exquisitely detailed flowers and petals, animals and birds, were rendered in a celebratory, distinctive style that was moody and rich, yet full of vitality. Even the dark and mysterious backgrounds appeared radiant. A stillness and gravity pervaded the art that was immediately at odds with the exuberant and showy detailing of petals and blooms.

It is this distinctive period and style that inspire this palette. In common with the backgrounds of the Dutch Master paintings, this combination has a dark and moody base, with dark plum rather than black providing a sombre tone. This rich ground is balanced with a sensual deep violet purple, delicate lilac, fresh eucalyptus leaf, a more vivid, verdant leaf green and white. The colors almost dance off each other—the richness of the heady purples is cut by the freshness of the minty greens and white. It is an exercise in restraint and balance that simultaneously feels lively and interesting.

The exacting use of white is crucial here as it is this sharpness that gives the palette a sense of modernity. Imagine a soft cream in its stead and you would have a much more classical and traditional mood.

- In this room, the palette is contained in the wallpapers and fabrics that dress the bed; all other elements are kept suitably restrained. However, these colors would also look absolutely beautiful as plain linens and less decorative fabrics.

- A sage green is used as an accent to color occasional chairs and the bedstead and this keeps the palette sympathetically balanced with no harsh jolts of contrast.

- This palette is purposely warm and dramatic so could radically lift the feel of a room where there is little light, or where a sense of theatricality is needed.

As the sun shifts on its axis and the days gradually shorten, an extraordinary explosion of color takes place on the moorlands of the British Isles. The soft bottle greens and whites of summer grasses and daisies are replaced by an astonishing carpet of amethyst and mulberry heathers, occasionally punctuated by the stinging sharpness of yellow gorse flowers.

A Cornish coastal path or a Yorkshire moor in early fall seem almost unrecognizable from their summer counterparts, so thickly clothed are they in these vibrant shades. Strident and strong, they color the landscape with artful confidence, celebrating the end of one season and the beginning of another. Nowhere is this more apparent than in the Scottish Highlands where, set against the darkness of fading bracken and ancient stone, these richly textured hues evoke misty mornings, the smoky smell of peat fires and the warm embrace of naturally dyed tweeds.

It is this precious moment in time that dictates this particular palette. A rich, almost cardinal purple; wild violet and heather; a sharp acid green and a warm stony gray come together in a rich autumnal mix. As always, the palette needs careful balancing, here between the two main characters, the heather purple

Highland heather

and the acid green. Match the tones equally so that they sit side by side without fighting — from there you can use shades derived from both to create your own heathery mix. Do not underestimate the importance of your neutral here: a soft gray will give a contemporary feeling or a bleached string color a more traditional country feel. Either will work beautifully.

- For definition, choose the darkest version of your chosen neutral. For added vivacity, you could use a dark purple or acid green to highlight and add depth.

- In this room, the palette is brought together on the wallpaper panels and drapes with texture bringing further depth to the scheme. Soft velvets and heathery tweeds echo the colors of the landscape.

- The sharp yellow of gorse flowers works brilliantly as a contrast tone here, sitting easily alongside both green and purple.

153

Mood board see pages 186-7

154

Heathery tweeds and velvets in rich violet and green with shades of stony gray offer the perfect balance of calm and dynamism.

Rich and opulent, this mix of luxurious shades is given an even more lavish sense of occasion with the use of cut velvets and brocades.

ROCOCO

Witty, playful, colorful and voluptuous, Rococo style sums up the somewhat frivolous nature of Louis XV's court in eighteenth-century France. The painter Fragonard immortalized the trysts and amorous pursuits of the A-list of the period in bedrooms, parlors and lavish rustic settings; the ornate decorative style of architecture and interiors was an exercise in ostentatious luxury and curvaceous glamour. As such, nothing could be further from the austere Neoclassical style that followed and by the early nineteenth century the word "rococo" was used colloquially to mean "old-fashioned". Similarly, in today's world, this style couldn't be further from the clean lines of minimalist modern interiors, but to consign it to the irrelevant pile would be to miss a trick. The Rococo color palette was richly dramatic and by employing a few subtle techniques one can infuse a room with its innate glamour and still be up to date.

This warm and embracing palette perfectly suits a bedroom but would work just as well in a formal country sitting or dining room. Taking its cue from the exuberant depictions of nature in many Rococo paintings, walls and furnishings luxuriate with blowsy florals and entwined motifs. The color combination features a dark and intriguing base, with a dark plum rather than black setting the slightly shadowy tone.

Shades of bottle green and a light eucalyptus gray-green provide contrast, a rich raspberry adds even more warmth and depth, while accents of sharp alchemilla yellow introduce yet more contrast and highlight—as such the whole is reminiscent of the *chiaroscuro* that Rococo painters loved so much.

Most of the colors come from within the same tonal family, somewhere mid-way between the darkest and lightest ends of each color's spectrum, making them easy and relaxing to live with. However there are sharp strokes of brightness from the acidic alchemilla and a soft white that illuminate and add depth. As usual, one can alter the mood with subtle changes.

■ Keep walls soft and neutral to produce a lighter mood, but take care to keep the balance of warmth.

■ This palette really works its magic in rooms that seem cold, with little natural light. Use warm rich tones of plum or eggplant on walls, allowing the color to be the focus of the room.

■ For a more contemporary look, increase the balance of alchemilla or introduce touches of fern green, gray and chalk white.

157

English country garden

Inspired by the romantic beauty of summer in an English garden, this palette uses shades from both sides of the color spectrum and a few in between to create a room that exudes serenity and vitality in equal measure. As always, it is the balance of these shades when used together that creates the harmony we all seem to crave in our homes.

The main color in the scheme is a strident, bold pink—an overtly positive and feminine shade—yet this color is not allowed to dominate the space. Its rich strength is sharpened and diffused, first by the chalky white of the drapes' linen ground and the plain linen sofa, then by the freshness of a soft watery jade and cool blue-gray.

The use of jade green here is crucial. Its minty freshness lends the scheme a lightness and delicacy where, say, a lime or bottle green would look either too zingy or too dull. It has a refined and elegant quality that somehow curtails the pink's potential shock factor.

The slate blue-gray grounds both colors, adding a serious, sophisticated note that edges the palette from frivolity to a more mature mood. With these three colors the palette is almost complete; now one can personalize and change the feeling of the scheme.

- Increase the volume of the pink— perhaps with the addition of a shocking pink cushion and throw, or a sumptuously patterned velvet chair— and you will also turn up the femininity and wow factor.

- Add more "battleship gray" and the femininity will recede against the intelligent neutrality—the scheme will feel more moody and mysterious.

- Increase the watery delicacy with further accents of soft jade and celadon and the space will feel dreamy and serene.

- A shot of turquoise silk would add glamour and punch, keeping things cooler while standing up to the power of the rose pink.

As the seasons shift and the bright light of summer is replaced by a golden autumnal glow, the colors around us take on a different personality. One can sense the move from summer to fall as a slight chill creeps into early mornings and evening edges in earlier every day. It is this transitional moment between seasons that inspired this distinctive palette of sophisticated warmth and depth. The colors are perfectly and carefully balanced between the rich shades of fall—plum, damson, heather, burnt orange and gray—and those of late summer—soft white, jade green, acacia with gentle dashes of indigo. It is this subliminal juxtaposition between cool and warm, strong and gentle that makes this timeless palette work so beautifully. Its versatility means it can easily be manipulated to suit different spaces and styles. For example the addition of cool tones will give a more tailored look in a light-filled room, whereas richer tones will warm up a cool space.

In this room, the palette's autumnal shades glow in the flowered drapes while a soft powdery gray colors the walls and rug. As the room is full of light a bright acacia-green silk curtain adds a sharp accent, but that and a velvet cushion in the same color and a single bright green chair are the only vivid notes in an otherwise richly tonal scheme.

fall bouquet

In a cold north-facing room one could easily change the green for a darker damson or warm russet for richness; or pick up the cool blue-gray of the background for a more sober feeling.

- Gray not black or graphite is the neutral of choice here. The right gray is vital to establish the tone you want in the overall scheme.

- The white used in this palette is also crucial—neither sharp nor bright but instead soft and mellow, a choice that subliminally adds warmth and harmony. A sharp bluish white would upset the delicate balance of the mix while this shade adds space, allowing the other colors to sing.

- Note how an accent color links to other details within the room to ensure a harmonious feel: here, the drapes link to a cushion and are picked up in vases and flowers.

Mood board see page 189

Just after the end of World War II a revolution took place in the world of fashion. After years of depression, rationing and shapeless clothes in dull fabrics, a spark of creativity and new energy burst from the haute couture studio of Christian Dior in Paris. Gone were the austere and functional fashions of the war years, to be replaced by a new-found elegance and femininity; a grace and extravagance that had not been seen for years. It was a lightning bolt moment—the birth of a new silhouette that became known as the New Look. Slightly curved shoulders, waspish waists and longer, fuller skirts became the shape that celebrated the female form and seemingly life itself. The moment was also one of daring and innovation as bright new fabrics were created and used with abandon.

It is this spirit of hope and renewal that inspired this particular palette. Indeed it is every bit as innovative as the New Look itself. What could be seen as clashing colors are in fact joyful—positive and celebratory with accents of daring feminine shades of rose and peony pink, marigold and sunshine yellow—used with a sharp white and an inky dark indigo that give an almost monochromatic base to the mix. It is a combination that signals optimism and confidence, capturing that feel-good spirit that set the world of fashion alight in 1947 and bringing it indoors.

Whilst the palette is undoubtedly pretty, it does not have to be sweet; balancing the femininity with inky blue adds strength and a dash of gravitas and reins in its girlish charm. Note the use of dark blue—as serious as black but without the heaviness and graphic without

fifties fashion

overpowering the fulsomeness of color. It is this tone that lends a neutral base and grounds the scheme. Also important is the white—quite sharp with a bluish base that feels crisp, bright and new.

- Stick to the same tones of the bright colors to ensure they don't fight among themselves. A too-bright pink could dominate the others and upset the balance.

- For a modern, contemporary feel let these colors sing out against this crisp blue-white base. To "age" the scheme, use a creamy, yellow-based white that will give the palette a vintage feel.

- If indigo doesn't appeal as a neutral a blue-based battleship gray could be a good alternative.

- In a north-facing room, this palette could be warmed up with the use of textures like wool, velvet and silk.

Mood board see page 189   171

Japanese blossom

Sometime between the months of March and May the gardens and parks of Japan take on breathtaking new life as spring marks the cherry blossom, or *sakura*, season. There is something truly enchanting about spring blossom: from the bitter cold and darkest bare branches of winter sprout magical, delicate clouds of softest pink. At first tiny buds appear, then blossom and grow until the somber boughs almost seem to groan under the weight of thousands of petals. It is uncannily romantic and joyful—at the same time, a reminder of the transitory nature and constantly evolving circle of life.

It is this exquisite moment in time that inspires this palette: elegant, feminine, with a serenity and delicacy that infuses a space with the ephemeral beauty of the *sakura* season.

Soft cloudy white is coupled with palest pink and layered with brighter pinks and a pale shade of leaf green, a mix that is almost impossibly pretty and romantic.

A dark graphite, the shade of cherry tree branches after winter, provides strength and sharpness: its graphic precision cuts the sweetness, whilst allowing just enough of the prettiness and nostalgia to shine through, albeit curtailed in modern monochrome.

- The delicacy of the scheme depends as much on the right white as it does on the shades of pink.

- The shades of pink are warm, containing little or no blue; this is vital to allow that powdery delicacy to work.

- Use the darkest graphite, but with care: it should simply rein in rather than dominate. Too much graphite and you will lose the grace and fragility of the scheme.

- To add definition, just use a deeper and stronger tone of pink; no stark contrasts or jolts of accent color here.

The 1950s in Rome was a supremely glamorous time: the post-war years finally saw Europe with a spring in its step and nowhere was this more keenly observed than in the Eternal City. Using Rome as an extraordinary backdrop, the new mood of elegance and stylish frivolity was perfectly captured by the Italian film director Federico Fellini in his iconic work *La Dolce Vita*, one of the most critically acclaimed films of all time. It is the glamorous and sophisticated lifestyle of that period that inspired this elegant and romantic palette.

Tones of black-and-white marble form the backbone to the scheme and echo Fellini's black-and-white photography. This is then softened with a romantic take of fifties rose pink, salvia green, shades of gray and touches of warm mysterious amber.

It is important to note that neither the black nor the white here are true representations, but rather shaded versions of these colors without the sharp harshness. A soft marble white and dark graphite represent crisp nostalgia

la dolce vita

without being overly dominant, allowing the softer, more romantic shades of pink and sage green to add frivolity and style. The use of amber adds depth and warmth to the mix.

- Increase the prettiness with more rose pink and soft white; building up the shades of gray will add more style and take the palette in a less feminine direction.

- Lighter silver and platinum grays increase the glamour value, especially when used in silky textures. For the opposite effect use darker toned gray linens or even wools for depth.

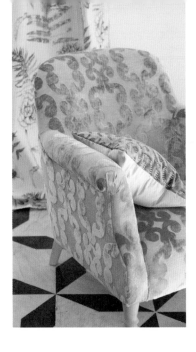

film star glamour

In this stylish and elegant drawing room, the palette is contained in the pattern that decorates walls and curtains. Its frothy exuberance is restrained by the black, white and gray elements, such as the floor and the softly shaded banner at the window. The whole is a brilliant balance of sophistication and femininity, exuberance and restraint.

India modern

From the misty mountain landscapes of the north to the impressive deserts and forts of Rajasthan or the sultry, verdant jungles of the south, India means different things to different people. But there is one thing that all lovers of India can agree upon and that is its ubiquitous, confident and sensational sense of color.

To many in the West, the combination of hot pink, sunshine yellow and spicy orange would be unthinkable, whereas India colors its everyday life with these shades (and many others) as easily and nonchalantly as if it were simply shrugging on a shawl. India is not afraid of getting it wrong. It knows. It understands that colors are like beats of a drum that resonate on a subliminal level and celebrate life itself.

In this palette some of my favorite Indian colors come together in a splendid fusion of femininity, daring, strength and dynamism. Shocking, hot pink, carmine red, turmeric and saffron mix with a rich eggplant, a stony gray and black—a combination that almost makes one's heart skip a beat. It is rich and uncompromising and, at first sight, more than a little daunting, but look closely and there are clever ways that make this sensational mix work anywhere. The stone colored natural is soft and offers a cool, neutral respite from the spicy warmth of the other colors—not so bright as to be white, which would upset the rhythm and flow of the other colors, but gentle enough to diffuse their power without taking away the intensity. The charcoal black, while being utterly authentic, adds a graphic edge of modernity and sharpens the heady strength of the warmer tones. Finally, the rich purple eggplant is in itself almost a neutral base, its dark moodiness allowing the other colors to sing against it, while maintaining a harmony that a cooler neutral such as green would not achieve.

- To make this palette work in any room one has to understand what each tone gives to the total mix. Use the stone, black and eggplant as your base, either individually or as a combination.

- This palette is not for the faint-hearted, so be confident: choose your combination of accent colors and let them color cushions and throws, drapes and pictures, linking the room together with each stroke of color. Repeat them, so that they become a language of their own—this will make the space feel cohesive.

palette directory

Designers Guild stock over 5,000 plain fabrics to choose from and many more patterns and weaves. Here, we have matched the colors in the book's palettes to one of our 154 paint colors and its matching *Parchment* plain wallpaper, and/or a plain fabric from either our *Brera Lino* linens or from one of our plain velvet collections— *Varese*, *Pavia* or *Cassia*. The symbols *p w* after a name indicates that this color is available both as a paint and a plain *Parchment* wallpaper; the fabric names are given in full.

White on white
page 13

Pure White *p w*
Brera Lino Oyster

Snowdrift *p w*
Cassia Chalk

Taj Mahal *p w*
Brera Lino Parchment

Whitewash *p w*
Brera Lino Grey

Winter Surf *p w*
Brera Lino Cloud

Quartz Grey *p w*
Brera Lino Smoke

Cool Marble *p w*
Brera Lino Alabaster

Polished Cement *p w*
Cassia Vanilla

Classic blue and white
page 17

Cobalt *p w*
Varese Cerulean

Bluebell *p w*
Brera Lino Cornflower

Alabaster *p w*
Brera Lino Alabaster

Prussian *p w*
Varese Cobalt

Cassia Turquoise

Eau de Nil *p w*
Brera Lino Aqua

Patrician *p w*
Brera Lino Pewter

Winter Surf *p w*
Brera Lino Pale Grey

Mount Fuji views
page 23

Lapis Lazuli *p w*
Varese Cobalt

Forget Me Not *p w*
Brera Lino Kingfisher

Indian Ocean *p w*
Varese Azure

Cold Embers *p w*
Cassia Zinc

Pure White *p w*
Brera Lino Oyster

London Dove *p w*
Varese Cloud

Appleton Grey *p w*
Varese Granite

Notting Hill Slate *p w*
Brera Lino Charcoal

Silk road blues
page 27

Pavia Cobalt
Brera Lino Ultra Marine

Moonlit Night *p w*
Brera Lino Marine

Cobalt *p w*
Varese Cobalt

Vintage Denim *p w*
Brera Lino Denim

Patrician *p w*
Brera Lino Mink

Whitewash *p w*
Brera Lino Oyster

Iron Ore *p w*
Brera Lino Woodsmoke

Marine *p w*
Pavia Ocean

Scandinavian cool
page 29

Moonlit Night *p w*
Brera Lino Denim

Vintage Denim *p w*
Brera Lino Marine

TG Green *p w*
Brera Lino Grass

Prussian *p w*
Brera Lino Lagoon

Appleton Grey *p w*
Brera Lino Dusk

Iron Ore *p w*
Brera Lino Granite

Winter Surf *p w*
Brera Lino Pale Grey

Chalk *p w*
Brera Lino Alabaster

Midsummer skies
page 31

Chalk *p w*
Brera Lino Oyster

Clear Sky *p w*
Varese Sky

Forget Me Not *p w*
Brera Lino Porcelain

Delft Tile *p w*
Varese Cerulean

Cloud *p w*
Varese Cloud

Green Apple *p w*
Brera Lino Grass

Brera Lino Primrose

Brera Lino Camellia

Winter landscape
page 37

Cloud *p w*
Brera Lino Duck Egg

Bayswater Blue *p w*
Varese Sky

Cloudless *p w*
Brera Lino Sky

Parsons Green *p w*
Brera Lino Celadon

Dawn Mist *p w*
Brera Lino Platinum

Brera Lino Apple

Brera Lino Camellia

Snow Drift *p w*
Cassia Chalk

Maiolica
page 41

Cloud *p w*
Brera Lino Pale Grey

Pure White *p w*
Brera Lino Oyster

Clear Sky *p w*
Varese Sky

Sainte Chapelle *p w*
Varese Cerulean

Varese Leaf *p w*
Varese Apple

Cornish Ware *p w*
Brera Lino Cobalt

Brera Lino Azalea

Brera Lino Camellia

Faded frescoes
page 47

Sainte Chapelle *p w*
Brera Lino Cobalt

Delft Tile *p w*
Brera Lino Cornflower

Forget Me Not *p w*
Varese Sky

Mauve Roses
Varese Crocus

Wild Violet
Cassia Lavender

Winter Surf *p w*
Cassia Zinc

Brera Lino Grass

Brera Lino Malachite

Persian minakari
page 51

Sainte Chapelle *p w*
Brera Lino Cobalt

Brera Lino Lagoon

Prussian *p w*
Brera Lino Ultra Marine

Brera Lino Leaf

Notting Hill Slate *p w*
Brera Lino Charcoal

Emerald *p w*
Cassia Emerald

Battleship Grey *p w*
Brera Lino Pewter

Chalk *p w*
Brera Lino Alabaster

Swedish Gustavian
page 57

Celadon *p w*
Brera Lino Pale Aqua

Duck Egg *p w*
Varese Aqua

Poivre Blanc *p w*
Brera Lino Alabaster

White Wash *p w*
Varese Chalk

Capisoli Grass

Moody Grey *p w*
Cassia Granite

Antique Jade *p w*
Varese Ocean

Gull's Wing *p w*
Brera Lino Silver

Venetian marbling
page 61

Moonlit Night *p w*
Cassia Denim

Brera Lino Malachite

Vintage Denim *p w*
Brera Lino Denim

Notting Hill Slate *p w*
Varese Mist

Cassia Turquoise

River Reed *p w*
Cassia Moss

Concrete *p w*
Cassia Zinc

Quartz Grey *p w*
Brera Lino Oyster

Arts and crafts
page 65

Gull's Wing *p w*
Brera Lino Silver

Moody Grey *p w*
Brera Lino Pewter

Appleton Grey *p w*
Brera Lino Granite

Varese Sea

Brera Lino Kingfisher

Cassia Ocean

Eau de Nil *p w*
Cassia Eau de Nil

Pavia Viola
Cassia Violet

Seashore
page 69

Silver Birch *p w*
Cassia Linen

Eucalyptus Leaf *p w*
Varese Duck Egg

Spring Mist *p w*
Cassia Celadon

Antique Jade *p w*
Cassia Eau de Nil

Artichoke *p w*
Varese Leaf

Steel *p w*
Cassia Zinc

Aqua *p w*
Varese Aqua

Winter Surf *p w*
Brera Lino Cloud

Celadon and jade
page 73

Gull's Wing *p w*
Brera Lino Silver

Celadon *p w*
Brera Lino Celadon

Fresh Mint *p w*
Brera Lino Aqua

Frozen Grape *p w*
Brera Lino Sea Mist

Thé Vert *p w*
Brera Lino Pistachio

Quartz Grey *p w*
Brera Lino Platinum

Cool Marble *p w*
Brera Lino Oyster

Eucalyptus Leaf *p w*
Varese Duck Egg

Reflections of China
page 77

Brera Lino Apple

Emerald *p w*
Brera Lino Thyme

Varese Leaf *p w*
Varese Apple

Greengage *p w*
Brera Lino Lime

Winter Surf *p w*
Brera Lino Cloud

Alchemilla *p w*
Brera Lino Alchemilla

Amalfi Lemon *p w*
Varese Alchemilla

Island Hibiscus *p w*
Varese Fuchsia

Modern botanical
page 81

Alabaster *p w*
Brera Lino Alabaster

Green Apple *p w*
Varese Apple

Trailing Willow *p w*
Varese Lime

Brera Lino Thyme

Vreeland Pink *p w*
Varese Cassis

Polished Cement *p w*
Brera Lino Silver

Iron Ore *p w*
Cassia Graphite

Brera Lino Primrose

Murano glass
page 83

Retro Jade *p w*
Brera Lino Pale Jade

Asparagus Fern *p w*
Brera Lino Moss

Cassia Turquoise

Glass Green *p w*
Cassia Eau de Nil

Spring Mist *p w*
Brera Lino Mist

Whitewash *p w*
Brera Lino Platinum

Cassia Grass

Dawn Mist *p w*
Brera Lino Platinum

Mid-century modern
page 87

Whitewash *p w*
Brera Lino Chalk

Gull's Wing *p w*
Brera Lino Cloud

Iron Ore *p w*
Cassia Graphite

Brera Lino Charcoal

Brera Lino Alchemilla

Green Apple *p w*

Parsons Green *p w*
Brera Lino Jade

Brera Lino Ivy

Umbria in spring
page 91

Giardino *p w*
Cassia Pear

Primrose *p w*

River Reed *p w*
Cassia Moss

Green Melon *p w*
Brera Lino Straw

Williams Pear *p w*

Snow Drift *p w*
Brera Lino Alabaster

Portobello Grey *p w*
Brera Lino Smoke

Soft Angelica *p w*
Brera Lino Dew

Brecon hills
page 93

Whitewash *p w*
Brera Lino Parchment

Silver Birch *p w*
Brera Lino Putty

Grey Pearl *p w*
Brera Lino Smoke

Tuscan Olive *p w*
Brera Lino Thyme

London Roof *p w*
Cassia Granite

Fenouil *p w*
Cassia Acacia

Brera Lino Leaf

Green Apple *p w*
Cassia Moss

Neutrals with zing
page 95

Chalk *p w*
Cassia Chalk

London Roof *p w*
Varese Granite

Cheviot Flannel *p w*
Brera Lino Pewter

Fenouil *p w*
Cassia Acacia

River Reed *p w*
Cassia Moss

Alchemilla *p w*
Cassia Acacia

Pebble *p w*
Cassia Dove

Varese Raven

Parisian chic
page 99

Quartz Grey *p w*
Brera Lino Pale Grey

Notting Hill Slate *p w*
Cassia Slate

Cheviot Flannel *p w*
Varese Granite

Cassia Acacia

Cassia Raven

Asparagus Fern *p w*
Cassia Acacia

Varese Alchemilla

Brera Lino Olive

Woodland spring
page 101

Winter Surf *p w*
Brera Lino Silver

Glass Green *p w*
Cassia Pear

Fenouil *p w*
Cassia Acacia

Primrose *p w*
Brera Lino Vanilla

Brera Lino Forest

Trailing Willow *p w*
Brera Lino Straw

Silver Birch *p w*
Cassia Linen

Brera Lino Granite

Summer sorbet
page 105

Snow Drift *p w*
Brera Lino Mink

Sugared Almond *p w*
Brera Lino Pale Rose

Venetian Lace *p w*
Brera Lino Straw

Panacotta *p w*
Brera Lino Vanilla

Brera Lino Pale Aqua

Aqua *p w*
Brera Lino Pale Jade

Brera Lino Dew

Frozen Grape *p w*
Brera Lino Pearl

Celebrating flowers
page 109

Purple Basil *p w*
Varese Grape

Cassia Fuchsia

Cassia Mist

Dawn Mist *p w*
Brera Lino Pale Grey

London Roof *p w*
Cassia Roebuck

Cassia Acacia

Brera Lino Thyme

Alabaster *p w*
Brera Lino Alabaster

Vintage roses
page 113

Portobello Grey *p w*
Cassia Dove

Polished Cement *p w*
Brera Lino Pale Grey

Snow Drift *p w*
Brera Lino Alabaster

Madame Butterfly *p w*
Brera Lino Peony

Sugared Almond *p w*
Brera Lino Pale Rose

Trailing Willow *p w*
Cassia Acacia

Fenouil *p w*
Varese Alchemilla

Tuscan Olive *p w*
Brera Lino Thyme

Vellum and parchment
page 117

Gull's Wing *p w*
Brera Lino Cloud

Chalk *p w*
Brera Lino Alabaster

Washed Linen *p w*
Brera Lino Calico

Custard Cream *p w*
Brera Lino Straw

Mother of Pearl *p w*
Brera Lino Pearl

Artichoke *p w*
Brera Lino Apple

Tuscan Olive *p w*
Brera Lino Thyme

Grey Pearl *p w*
Brera Lino Smoke

Irish linen
page 119

Autumn Hydrangea *p w*
Varese Viola

Tuscan Olive *p w*
Brera Lino Thyme

Frozen Grape *p w*
Brera Lino Dew

Grey Pearl *p w*
Brera Lino Pewter

Autumn Moor *p w*
Brera Lino Pebble

Concrete *p w*
Brera Lino Pale Grey

Winter Surf *p w*
Brera Lino Dove

Brera Lino Thistle

Italian marble
page 121

Concrete *p w*
Brera Lino Cloud

Pebble *p w*
Varese Linen

Portobello Grey *p w*
Varese Zinc

Pale Birch *p w*
Cassia Cameo

Poivre Blanc *p w*
Brera Lino Putty

Morning Frost *p w*
Brera Lino Platinum

Quartz Grey *p w*
Cassia Chalk

Gull's Wing *p w*
Brera Lino Pale Grey

Modern monochrome
page 125

Notting Hill Slate *p w*
Brera Lino Noir

Iron Ore *p w*
Cassia Slate

Patrician *p w*
Varese Granite

Appleton Grey *p w*
Brera Lino Granite

Moody Grey *p w*
Brera Lino Pewter

Dawn Mist *p w*
Brera Lino Cloud

Cool Marble *p w*
Brera Lino Alabaster

Alabaster *p w*
Brera Lino Oyster

Black+white = gray
page129

Notting Hill Slate *p w*
Brera Lino Noir

Iron Ore *p w*
Brera Lino Pewter

Varese Granite

Battleship Grey *p w*
Cassia Granite

Concrete *p w*
Brera Lino Pale Grey

Gull's Wing *p w*
Brera Lino Cloud

Pure White *p w*
Brera Lino Alabaster

Morning Frost *p w*
Brera Lino Graphite

London skyline
page 133

Cocoa Bean *p w*
Brera Lino Espresso

London Roof *p w*
Cassia Slate

Pale Graphite *p w*
Varese Granite

Polished Cement *p w*
Brera Lino Pale Grey

Chalk *p w*
Cassia Chalk

Silver Birch *p w*
Cassia Dove

Quartz Grey *p w*
Brera Lino Cloud

Alabaster *p w*
Brera Lino Alabaster

Winter smoke
page 135

Pavia Graphite

Notting Hill Slate *p w*
Varese Granite

Appleton Grey *p w*
Brera Lino Pewter

Cardamon Pod *p w*
Cassia Apple

Soft Angelica *p w*
Cassia Pear

London Dove *p w*
Varese Cloud

Whitewash *p w*
Cassia Chalk

Pure White *p w*
Brera Lino Alabaster

Colors of silence
page 139

Pavia Teal

Mauve Roses *p w*
Pavia Viola

Highland Heather *p w*
Brera Lino Iris

Dawn Mist *p w*
Brera Lino Cloud

Moody Grey *p w*
Brera Lino Pewter

Cirrus Cloud *p w*
Brera Lino Pale Grey

Polished Cement *p w*
Brera Lino Chalk

Whitewash *p w*

Old Provence
page 147

Leaden Pink *p w*
Varese Crocus

Mulberry Crush *p w*
Varese Viola

Chiffon Grey *p w*
Brera Lino Cameo

Morning Frost *p w*
Brera Lino Platinum

Cold Embers *p w*
Brera Lino Dove

Battleship Grey *p w*
Brera Lino Dusk

Mauve Roses *p w*
Brera Lino Heather

Star Sapphire *p w*
Brera Lino Iris

Dutch flowers
page 149

Purple Basil *p w*
Brera Lino Thistle

Autumn Moor *p w*
Brera Lino Currant

Wild Violet *p w*
Brera Lino Iris

Mauve Roses *p w*
Varese Crocus

Cardamon Pod *p w*
Brera Lino Apple

Tuscan Olive *p w*
Brera Lino Thyme

Steel *p w*
Brera Lino Pale Grey

Fenouil *p w*
Varese Lime

Highland heather
page 153

Purple Basil *p w*
Pavia Aubergine

Mauve Roses *p w*
Pavia Viola

Tuscan Olive *p w*
Brera Lino Jade

Asparagus Fern *p w*
Brera Lino Moss

Moody Grey *p w*
Brera Lino Smoke

Gull's Wing *p w*
Brera Lino Silver

Quartz Grey *p w*
Varese Chalk

Iron Ore *p w*
Varese Zinc

Rococo
page 157

Melanzane *p w*
Brera Lino Aubergine

Autumn Hydrangea *p w*
Brera Lino Thistle

Pale Birch *p w*
Cassia Dove

Poivre Blanc *p w*
Cassia Linen

Vreeland Pink *p w*
Varese Fuchsia

Cardamon Pod *p w*
Varese Leaf

Snowdrift *p w*
Brera Lino Cloud

River Reed *p w*
Brera Lino Moss

English country garden
page 161

Whitewash *p w*
Brera Lino Parchment

Moody Grey *p w*
Cassia Zinc

Iron Ore *p w*
Cassia Granite

Celadon *p w*
Brera Lino Celadon

Eucalyptus Leaf *p w*
Varese Duck Egg

Brera Lino Thyme

Island Hibiscus *p w*
Varese Fuchsia

Brera Lino Scarlet

Fall bouquet
page 163

Vreeland Pink *p w*
Varese Fuchsia

Cassia Ocean

Cassia Emerald

Battleship Grey *p w*
Brera Lino Pewter

Dawn Mist *p w*
Brera Lino Graphite

Gull's Wings *p w*
Cassia Zinc

Cassia Currant

Spring Mist *p w*
Cassia Celadon

Fifties fashion
page 169

Chalk *p w*
Brera Lino Parchment

Morning Frost *p w*
Brera Lino Putty

Notting Hill Slate *p w*
Cassia Graphite

Cassia Acacia

Giardino *p w*
Varese Leaf

Cassia Kingfisher

Varese Fuchsia

Brera Lino Scarlet

Japanese blossom
page 173

Pure White *p w*
Brera Lino Oyster

Whitewash *p w*
Brera Lino Alabaster

Pink Porcelain *p w*
Brera Lino Pearl

First Blush *p w*
Varese Pale Rose

Brera Lino Camellia

London Dove *p w*
Brera Lino Graphite

Brera Lino Apple

Brera Lino Woodsmoke

La dolce vita
page 177

Alabaster *p w*
Brera Lino Alabaster

Faded Blossom *p w*
Varese Crocus

Vreeland Pink *p w*
Varese Cassis

Appleton Grey *p w*
Brera Lino Pewter

Iron Ore *p w*
Varese Mist

Pavia Teal

Brera Lino Thyme

Brera Lino Charcoal

India modern
page 181

Cassia Ocean

Cassia Eau de Nil

Cassia Damson

Cassia Fuchsia

Iron Ore *p w*
Brera Lino Granite

Cheviot Flannel *p w*
Brera Lino Zinc

Portobello Grey *p w*
Brera Lino Pale Grey

Taj Mahal *p w*

mood
boards
key

Creating a mood board is a great way to start on a new scheme. Bringing together all your chosen elements—fabrics, wallpapers, paints and inspiration—allows you to see the relationships and balance of shades and tones of colors, textures and patterns, to get a good idea of how well a room is going to work. Make sure you put your sample pieces on the board in the same scale as they will be in the room. Include objects or photographs that have inspired you, to keep your ideas focused. If it works on paper it will work in your room!

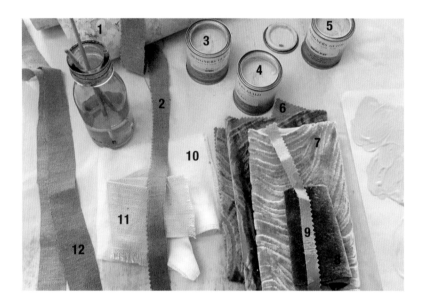

Foreword page 4

1 Lustro
2 Padua Turquoise
3 Steel paint
4 Fresh Mint paint
5 Spring Mist paint
6 Aurelia Grass
7 Aurelia Duck Egg
8 Pavia Ocean
9 Majella Leaf
10 Brera Lino Alabaster
11 Brera Lino Sea Mist
12 Pavia Grass

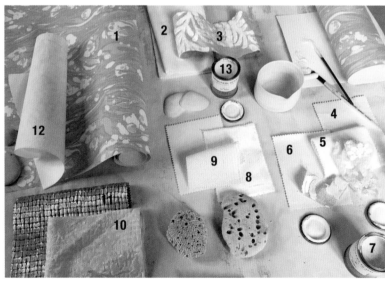

White on white page 10

1 Delahaye
2 Pavia Chalk
3 Zanfirico Chalk
4 Canvas Ivory
5 Varese Chalk
6 Canvas Alabaster
7 Cool Marble paint
8 Pavia Chalk
9 Chiron Chalk
10 Boratti Bianco
11 Castellani Chalk
12 Ecru Lustro wallpaper
13 Taj Majal paint

Maiolica page 44

1 Majolica Cornflower
2 Majolica Cornflower wallpaper
3 Iridato Sky
4 Lustro Cerulian
5 Murrine Delft
6 Quartz Grey paint
7 Sainte Chapelle paint
8 Brera Lino Alabaster
9 Brera Lino Azalea

Swedish Gustavian page 58

1 Floreale Celadon wallpaper
2 Floreale Grande Celadon
3 Pugin Zinc
4 Pugin Emerald
5 Padua Duck Egg
6 Pugin Ocean
7 Chiron Chalk
8 Cassia Celadon
9 Aalter Zinc
10 Salvia paint
11 Verdigris paint
12 Celadon paint
13 Waterleaf paint

Mid-century modern page 89

1 Delahaye Emerald wallpaper
2 Brecon Emerald
3 Varese Leaf
4 Trailing Willow paint
5 Delahaye Emerald
6 Brecon Ebony
7 Brecon Absinthe
8 Roxburgh Moss
9 Pavia Fir
10 Cassia Grass

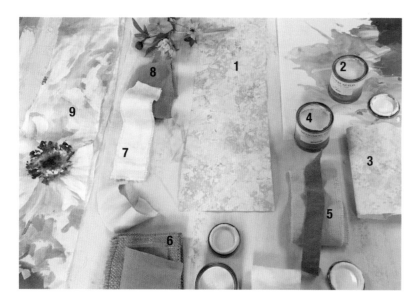

Summer sorbet   page 106

1 Lustro Birch wallpaper
2 Taj Mahal paint
3 Lustro Birch
4 Primrose paint
5 Brera Lino Sea Mist
6 Aalter Zinc
7 Brera Lino Vanilla
8 Brera Lino Celadon
9 Palissy Grande Camellia

Colors of silence   page 142

1 Marianne Viola
2 Chiffon Grey paint
3 Patrician paint
4 Cirrus Cloud paint
5 Pavia Chalk
6 Majella Platinum
7 Polished Cement paint
8 Marianne Viola wallpaper
9 Brera Lino Sea Mist
10 Brera Lino Duck Egg
11 Brera Lino Alabaster
12 Pavia Ocean
13 Pavia Zinc

Highland heather   page 154

1 Aubriet Amethyst
2 Majella Leaf
3 Majella Crocus
4 Purple Basil paint
5 Patrician paint
6 Green Apple paint
7 Aubriet Amethyst
8 Corneille Amethyst
9 Bentham Moss
10 Pavia Leaf
11 Melville Moss
12 Pavia Acacia

Fall bouquet page 165

1 Marianne Fuchsia
2 Patrician paint
3 Marianne Fuchsia wallpaper
4 Green Apple paint
5 Tuscan Olive paint
6 Gulls Wing paint
7 Santicelli Leaf
8 Melville Magenta
9 Roxburgh Fuchsia
10 Brera Lino Alabaster
11 Roxburgh Zinc
12 Majella Viridian

Fifties fashion page 171

1 Couture Rose Fuchsia wallpaper
2 Couture Rose
3 Aurelia Chalk
4 Brera Lino Oyster
5 Majella Fuchsia
6 Padua Slate
7 Notting Hill Slate paint
8 Eglantine Tuberose

La dolce vita page 179

1 Majolica Slate
2 Brera Lino Alabaster
3 Brera Lino Zinc
4 Latticino Graphite
5 Majolica Slate wallpaper
6 Murrine Crocus
7 Brera Lino Dusk
8 Iridato Peony
9 Chalk paint

Designers Guild Stockists

Designers Guild Home Accessories are available from selected retailers throughout the US and Canada. To find your local stockist, please visit

www.designersguild.com/stockist

North America Designers Guild Flagship Trade Showroom for Bed, Bath & Accessories
230 5th Avenue, Suite 1903
New York City, New York 10001
Tel: 212 967 4540

Designers Guild Fabrics & Wallpapers are available through interior decorators and designers throughout the US and Canada, distributed by Osborne & Little Inc. They are available through the following trade showrooms.

U.S.A.

Dean Warren 2716 N. 68th Street, Suite 1, Scottsdale, Arizona 85257   Tel: 480 990 9233

Osborne & Little, Inc. 101 Henry Adams Street, Suite 435, San Francisco, California 94103
Tel: 415 255 8987

Osborne & Little, Inc. Pacific Design Center, 8687 Melrose Avenue, Suite B643, Los Angeles, California 90069   Tel: 310 659 7667

Shanahan Collection Denver Design Center, 595 S. Broadway, Suite 105W, Denver, Colorado 80209   Tel: 303 778 7088

Osborne & Little, Inc. 90 Commerce Road, Stamford, Conneticut 6902   Tel: 203 359 1500

Osborne & Little, Inc. 1099 14th Street NW, Suite 320 Washington DC, Virginia 20025
Tel: 202 554 8800

Ammon Hickson, Inc. 1855 Griffin Road, Suite B364, Dania Beach, Florida   Tel: 954 925 1555

Ainsworth Noah 351 Peachtree Hills Avenue, Suite 507, Atlanta, Georgia 30305
Tel: 404 231 8787

Osborne & Little, Inc. Merchandise Mart, Suite 610, Chicago, Illinois 60654
Tel: 312 467 0913

Designers Only 5225 W. 75th Street, Prairie Village, Kansas City, Kansas 66208
Tel: 913 649 3778

Osborne & Little The Boston Design Centre, 1 Design Center Place, Suite 551, Boston, Massachusetts 2210   Tel: 617 737 2927

Design & Detail 2731 Sutton Boulevard, Suite 100, Maplewood, St Louis, Missouri 63143 Tel: 314 781 3336

M/R Design Lab 4815 W. Russell Road, Suite 2B, Las Vegas, Nevada 89178   Tel: 702 202 4550

Floor Décor and Design 6801 Jericho Turnpike, Syosset, New York 11791   Tel: 516 864 0027

Osborne & Little Inc. 979 Third Avenue, Suite 520, New York City, New York 10022 Tel: 212 751 3333

Gregory Alonso Ohio Design Center, 23533 Mercantile Road, Suite 113, Beachwood, Cleveland, Ohio 44122   Tel: 216 765 1810

The Baer Collection Showroom at the Witherspoon Building 130 South Juniper Street, Suite 307, Philadelphia, Pennsylvania 19107 Tel: 215 568 6980

I.D Collection 1025 N. Stemmons Frwy, Suite 745, Dallas, Texas 75207 Tel: 214 698 0226

I.D. Collection 5120 Woodway Drive, Suite 4001, Houston, Texas 77056   Tel: 713 623 2344

The Dixon Group 5701 6th Avenue South, The Seattle Design Center, Plaze Suite 162, Seattle, Washington 98108   Tel: 206 767 4454

Canada

Primavera 160 Pears Ave. Suite 110, Toronto, Ontario M5R 3P8 Tel: 416 921 3334

Central & South America

Argentina Miranda Green

Dominican Republic Casa Kyrez

Brazil Beraldin Textiles

Chile Importaciones Santa Cuz Limitada

Colombia Denise Webb Textiles

Ecuador Home Indentity

Mexico Artell

Panama Metropolitan Furniture S.A.

Peru Romantex S.A.

Uruguay Nicole Hernstadt

Venezuela Idea 58 C.A.

Designers Guild products are available in over 80 countries around the world. For full details on all of our agents and distributors please visit our website.

Acknowledgments

I would like to thank my brilliant team without whom this book would not have been possible: Alison Cathie, Anne Furniss, Amanda Back, Jo Willer, Meryl Lloyd and James Merrell.

To all the team at Designers Guild for such wonderful support.

We would like to thank the following designers and organizations for kind permission to reproduce images of their work:
Author photograph page 7 and back cover Bernard Touillon.
Moodboard photography by Jo Willer.

With many thanks to
Roxy Klassik for loaning us some of their classic Scandinavian furniture. www.roxyklassik.dk
Jonas & Christine Juel Bjerre-Poulsen for allowing us to photograph in their beautiful apartment.
GETAMA who still produce the iconic Hans Wegner daybed at their factory in Gedsted. www.getama.dk

Every effort has been made at the time of going to press to trace the copyright holders, architects and designers whose work appears in this book. We apologize for any unintentional omission and would be pleased to insert the appropriate acknowledgment in any subsequent edition.

Text: Amanda Back
Stylist: Jo Willer
Project Editor: Anne Furniss
Design: Meryl Lloyd
Photography: James Merrell

Publishing Director: Sarah Lavelle
Creative Director: Helen Lewis
Production: Stephen Lang, Vincent Smith

First published in 2017 by Quadrille Publishing Ltd
Pentagon House, 52–54 Southwark Street,
London SE1 1UN
www.quadrille.co.uk | www.quadrille.com
Quadrille Publishing is an imprint of Hardie Grant
www.hardiegrant.com.au

Text © 2017 Quadrille Publishing Ltd
Photography © James Merrell
Design and layout © 2017 Quadrille Publishing Ltd

Cataloguing-In-Publication Data: A catalogue record for this book is available from the British Library.

ISBN 978 184949 990 3

10 9 8 7 6 5 4 3 2 1

Printed in China

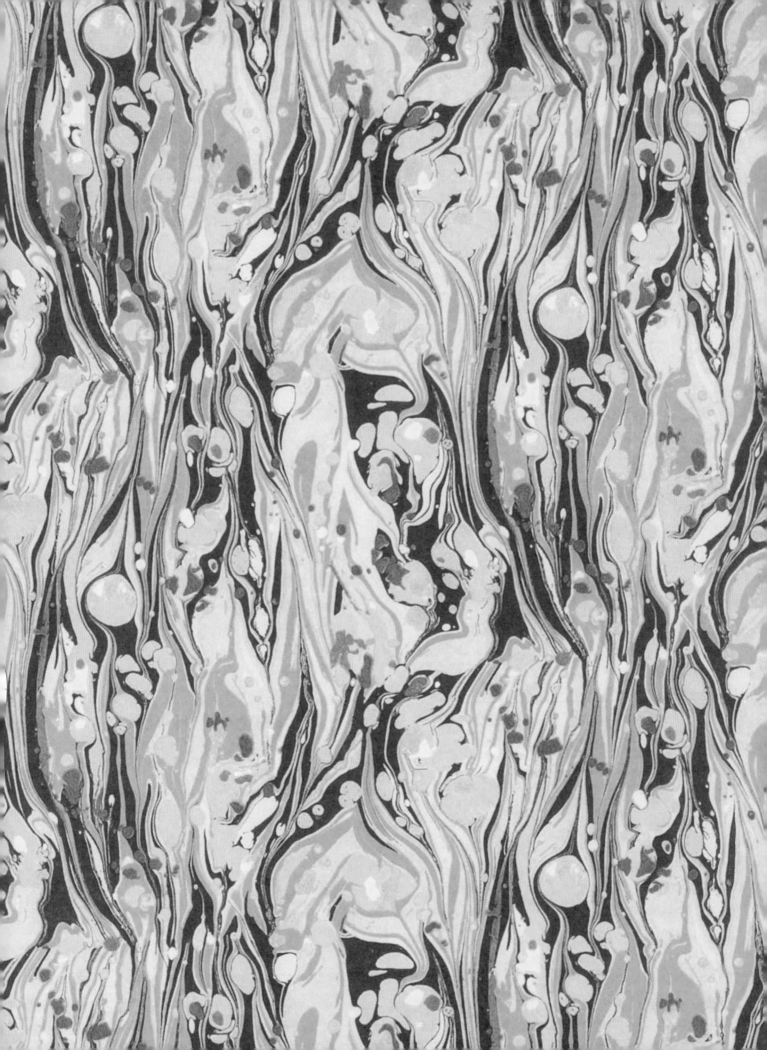